# A TWINKLE AT THE END

# A Twinkle at the End

ALAN O'HASHI

# Contents

# Dedication

I've made it through seven decades, heading into my eighth, and along the way, I've gathered stories, scars, and insights that have shaped my understanding of life. I dedicate *A Twinkle at the End* to those who are younger than me—not as a lecture, but as a cautionary tale. The journey through our healthcare system has often felt less like being cared for and more like surviving what I call the "health scare" system. What was once intended to promote wellness has, in many ways, become a complex web of high costs, difficult choices, and fear-driven narratives.

Depending on the reports you read, Generation X and the Millennials may be the first generations in modern history to face a shorter life expectancy than their Baby Boomer elders. That reality alone should give pause. While many in those generations are vibrant and healthy, far too many find themselves struggling with obesity, brought on by processed foods, rushed meals, and the merging of home life with the demands of a relentless, fast-paced work culture. To that burden add the misuse of drugs and alcohol, sometimes to escape stress, sometimes to fill emotional gaps, and you see how the challenges stack up.

Life expectancy is about more than diet and lifestyle choices. Economic pressures weigh heavily, especially for Gen-Xers and Millennials. Many of them pursued college because they were told it was the surest path to stability, only to find themselves saddled with mountains of student debt and working jobs that often don't require the degrees they earned. Others juggle multiple part-time positions, patching together income at the expense of stability, benefits, and peace of mind.

These stressors compound over time and inevitably impact both physical and mental health.

If the younger generations do manage to live long lives, they may not find their later years any easier than Baby Boomers or the Silent Generation before them. Rising healthcare costs, inadequate safety nets, and a lack of affordable housing for seniors loom large. The cycle threatens to repeat itself, leaving future generations with the same insecurities that plague us now.

This dedication is not written in despair. I write it with hope and gratitude. Through my own life, I have been lifted time and again by creative communities that nourished my spirit, even when the healthcare system tested my patience and resilience. I am thankful for the many writers who joined me in Shut Up & Write groups, gatherings that connected people across time zones and continents. Those sessions, especially the hearty crew of early risers who met from 5:30 to 7:30 a.m. seven days a week, shaped me into the writer I am today. I no longer attend those groups, but the friendships, encouragement, and accountability are some of the brightest sparks in my writing life. During the uncertainty of the COVID-19 pandemic, these circles of creativity became more than writing groups. They were creative lifelines when I had to put my documentary filmmaking on hold.

To the younger generations: take this book as both a warning and an encouragement. Learn from the paths we walk, but don't be afraid to find new ones. To the writers, friends, and fellow travelers who have kept me company on this journey, know that this twinkle at the end shines a little brighter because of you.

# Prologue: Life Lived Backward

*A Twinkle at the End: Rewinding My Life Through America's Healthcare Maze* is my memoir, spanning seven, going on eight decades. My life, or at least the way I've chosen to tell it, runs backward. I collapsed while loading the dishwasher and was stone-cold dead.

It could have been bloodier.

I was about to place my big sushi knife in the utensil holder, blade up, when I landed on the open door. Instead, the Ginsu clattered harmlessly to the floor. That would have made for an exciting first sentence.

*A Twinkle at the End* is much like *The Curious Case of Benjamin Button* (1922), the short story by F. Scott Fitzgerald. Upon my death, a weird thing happens. I'm reborn but in my old body with achy, stiff joints and chronic pain. From there, I grow younger with each chapter. My body sheds its years while my story gathers the weight of everything that came before.

In Fitzgerald's tale, Benjamin Button ages in reverse until he dwindles into infancy. My story follows a similar arc. I start in the body of an old man who has seen too much of hospitals and waiting rooms, and I move backward through the pain, the confusion, the triumphs, and the losses. By the time I arrive at the end, I will be back at the beginning: an infant again, but one who remembers what it was like to grow old.

*A Twinkle at the End* also has elements of *A Christmas Carol* (1843), the novel by Charles Dickens. Like Scrooge, the Ghosts of Christmases Past, Present, and those Yet to Come visit me as I evaluate my life story, moving from rebirth, getting the pain of death out of the way, and living in reverse until a big finish with a happy ending.

I've been thinking about aging and have recounted some of my life experiences in the context of the American healthcare industrial complex paradox (That's a lot of Xs). Public and private healthcare companies dedicate themselves to keeping people alive and free from disease, but at the same time, they must also generate financial profits and sustain themselves. Nonprofit healthcare providers can generate revenue, but the IRS code prohibits the distribution of dividends to owners and stockholders.

Meanwhile, the industry keeps its heart thumping and pumping based on continually expanding the number of patients who consume pharmaceuticals, visit doctors, and are tested by new machines. It's better that people stay a little bit sick than be cured, at least from a profit and loss standpoint.

Fixing people up was a compassionate "loss leader," meaning medical care was offered at a price below its market value, resulting in a loss of revenue for the doctor or hospital. The sale of high-margin items, such as drugs, made up for the lost money. The primary business purpose of a loss leader is to attract customers, with the expectation that they will purchase higher-margin items. Healthcare was viewed as a "public good" until the for-profit motive changed healthcare service delivery.

Before private health insurance companies were mega-greedy, medical doctors were specialized shopkeepers. TV doctors like Marcus Welby and Dr. Kildare dealt with patients who walked through the door and served them more like retail customers. Doctors saw a certain number of patients per day, provided follow-up advice as needed, and made daily hospital rounds to check on patients who required more than routine care.

If the unseen powers of the universe miraculously healed all sick Americans, the national economy would collapse. The government wouldn't be able to print money fast enough to bail out the healthcare industrial complex while it waited for more people to get sick. The domino effect would be worse than when Wall Street bankers overextended themselves in 2008.

Now that I'm elderly and have found myself sucked into hospitals and doctors' offices more than ever, I've grown distrustful of them. Based on a healthcare emergency in 2013, I'm now uncertain whether they make decisions that are in my best interests. I could have benefited from additional healthcare and financial advocacy.

The squeaky patient gets the bedpan. I've learned that going to the Emergency Room (ER) in an ambulance increased my chances of being admitted to the hospital by the ER doctors. Movies and TV shows have depicted ambulances and ERs as reserved for emergencies like car accident victims and assessing casualties from mass shootings.

What if there were an Emergency Department and a Primary Care Department? These days, the term 'Emergency Department' is a misnomer. The ER is the first point of contact for any insured or uninsured patient, whether the visit is emergency or not, who hopes to be admitted to the hospital.

Some hospitals have claimed they are going broke because uninsured patients use the ERs as their primary medical care service providers, or as I call it, ER-gent Care. I've read that the insured and uninsured use the ER at generally the same rate.

For the insured, most Primary Care Physicians (PCP) don't have hospital admitting privileges and send their patients to the ER, where they take a number and get in line behind the heart attacks and gunshot wounds. If you broke an ankle, fell from a ladder changing a light bulb, or have a 101-degree temperature with flu-like symptoms, the wait can be several hours.

I caught myself up in the non-emergency versus emergency ER conundrum. My most memorable bout with the healthcare system was when I was in denial about the gravity of a 2013 illness that slowed me down for six months. I didn't think I was sick to the point I needed extraordinary medical care since I wasn't shot or having a heart attack, as the popular media had led me to believe. Kaiser Permanente (KP) is a nonprofit Health Maintenance Organization (HMO).

When I was on my college debate team in the mid-1970s, the question was whether a national healthcare insurance system would be better than the status quo. HMOs were a standard Affirmative Case because they were a successful early example of managed care. Managed care ultimately proved to be the most efficient way to deliver healthcare services in the 21st century.

I made an appointment with my PCP, Dr. Lookner, and stood naked, giving him a first-hand view of my skin and bones. He was empathetic but powerless to admit me to the hospital.

I returned home half-dead. It wasn't cancer or Alzheimer's, so I figured I was good. Besides, all I could do was moan and groan on the couch and hope to be less miserable. That night was unbearable, and I had to be driven to the ER. I sat in the waiting area for hours and was finally wheeled into a treatment room, only to be sent home by the night shift doctor as "not sick enough."

The next day, I was three-quarters dead, called 911, and returned to the hospital by ambulance. This time, the daytime ER doctor reviewed my chart from the night before, gave me the once-over, and admitted me into the hospital, where I stayed for a month.

I didn't see my PCP during my time in the hospital and rehab. These days, specialized "hospitalist" doctors manage and coordinate a patient's care while they are in the hospital. They also act as a liaison between the patient and their PCP. Gone are the days of Dr. Welby making hospital rounds.

So far, my life has been lucky when facing life-and-death situations. Over seven decades, I've had four close calls with death. The most recent was for emergency abdominal surgery in November and December 2023 after an ambulance took me off a cruise ship in Panama City, Panama.

At last check, according to the Social Security Administration actuary chart, I have 10.4 years to go, which means I will be dead when I'm 79. The next meet-up I have with the Grim Reaper will likely be the last. We all have unique experiences as we move through life. Being at the top of my game has been hard work. I'd rather have a positive influence on others I meet rather than a negative one. Will knowing my past behaviors make my life easier?

Alan O'Hashi
Boulder, Colorado

# Chapter 1

# The Living End: Un-dead and Medicare

We'll all be dead eventually. Death becomes more certain as we age. Pushing the physical and startling pain out of the way at the get-go would be the way to end and begin. What if an omniscient observer gave me a choice to live life backward by first starting dead, but reborn?

In 2042, I was 89, and still managing to take a few steps by walking from my condo to the Silver Sage Village (SSV) Common House office, where I wrote for three or four hours every morning.

I was still on a low dose of steroids for my arthritic hands. The stiffness and pain slowed my typing. That was good because my foggy brain could keep up with my slowed-down fingers. My last physically miserable 10 years haven't been very productive. I could still walk, and my long-term memory was good.

"Has anyone seen my keys?" The short-term was starting to go.

I advise everyone to get the pain of death out of the way at birth. Like anyone too young to die old, I've had all kinds of experiences. This time around, I'll be living in reverse. My last story, also the first in my new life, is about my encounters with the American healthcare system. A more accurate description would be the health-scare system.

I've been on Medicare since turning 65 in 2018. My long-time health insurance provider, Kaiser Permanente (KP), was still a free-standing nonprofit company and hadn't been acquired by a multinational corporation. Nonprofit businesses don't distribute profits to stockholders. No for-profit health-care provider would be interested in merging with KP. Even if KP went out of business, nonprofits are required to distribute their assets to other nonprofits with a similar mission.

*******

Last week, I went to the clinic for my annual combined flu/pneumonia/COVID-42 vaccination. While waiting for my turn, I picked up the *Aging Gratefully* magazine from the end table and read about my favorite President, Harry S. Truman, who took over when Franklin Roosevelt died in his fourth term. I became aware of Truman not because he ended World War II by ordering the atomic bombing of Nagasaki and Hiroshima, but on a positive note, he proposed a federally funded health insurance program three times between 1945 and 1949.

Powerful medical industry lobby interests, including the American Medical Association and the American Hospital Association, stalled his ideas from Congressional consideration because they reeked of "socialized medicine." For similar reasons, Congress nixed Roosevelt's New Deal national health insurance plan from the Social Security Act of 1935.

Medicare, initially known as the Dependents' Medical Care Act, provided healthcare for past and present members of the U.S. military and their families, and was passed during the Dwight D. Eisenhower administration in 1956. In 1961, Eisenhower convened the White House Conference on Aging, which resulted in a proposal establishing a healthcare program for Social Security beneficiaries.

*******

I finished my memoir prologue. "Remember to take your medicine with your meal," my digital assistant, Alexa, reminded me through the speaker in her black abode, sitting on my desk. I walked from my office in the SSV Common House to my condo to take a break. It was a handy commute.

My hands were sore but not painful enough to prevent me from boiling a can of chicken noodle soup, which hit the spot on a chilly fall afternoon. I brought the *Aging Gratefully* magazine home and finished reading the Truman article because I wanted to add a chapter about Medicare. I was only suitable for one serving, so I placed the rest in the fridge for later.

The door on my Amana swung closed. I opened the dishwasher to add my soup bowl when I instantly went down like a rock. That was a relief. I hoped reincarnation was an urban legend and wouldn't have to come back and watch *I Love Lucy* reruns, to paraphrase Woody Allen.

Just before the brain aneurysm, I flashed back to 1964 when I started collecting political memorabilia and plucked an "LBJ for the USA" cardboard placard stapled on a telephone pole by the newspaper office on East 17th Street in downtown Cheyenne. Back then, I liked Lyndon Johnson because he had to hit the ground running after a lone gunman, and maybe abetted by others, assassinated John Kennedy.

Johnson finished much of Kennedy's agenda when he signed an amendment to the Social Security Act establishing the Centers for Medicare and Medicaid Services. A payroll tax, beneficiary premiums, surtaxes from beneficiaries, co-pays, deductibles, and the U.S. Treasury combined to fund Medicare. Before Medicare was established, approximately 60 percent of people over 65 had some form of health insurance coverage.

Older adults paid more than three times as much for private health insurance as younger individuals.

Medicaid provides health coverage for low-income people. Unlike Medicare, each state administers its Medicaid program differently and can modify benefits. Medicaid is funded jointly by the federal government and the states. The federal government pays the Federal Medical Assistance Percentage (FMAP) of the total costs, while the states cover the remainder. Each state's average per capita income serves as the basis for the FMAP.

The Medicare and Medicaid signing ceremony occurred on July 30, 1965, at the Harry S. Truman Presidential Library in Independence, Missouri. The former President and his wife, Bess, became the program's first recipients after President Johnson signed the legislation into law.

Medicare later included eligible younger people disabled by terminal kidney illnesses and Lou Gehrig's disease. When I qualified for Medicare in 2018, the program insured over 52 million people aged 65 and older, as well as 8 million individuals younger than 65.

Original Medicare comprised four Parts: Part A covered hospital, skilled nursing, and hospice services, while Part B covered outpatient services. Part D covered self-administered prescription drugs. Part C was approved later as an alternative that offered a privatized approach, allowing patients to choose private insurance plans that provided the same services as Parts A and B, along with additional benefits.

Part C was first known as Medicare+Choice and was signed into law by President Bill Clinton in 1997. The U.S. House of Representatives impeached Clinton. The Senate acquitted him before the 105th Congress convened. The Republicans had taken control of the House and Senate and proposed a "private" option for public Medicare, later known as Medicare Advantage.

The Balanced Budget Act of 1997 cut Medicare expenses by spreading the risks to the private sector. Anyone who thinks a national insurance plan would cut out private insurers hasn't been on Medicare. In my view, the federal government lacks the necessary infrastructure to provide national insurance and would likely offer something similar to Medicare Advantage.

One of the unintended positive consequences of Part C was racial integration. The Civil Rights Act of 1965 conditionally made payments to Medicare and Medicaid providers in exchange for integrating thousands of waiting rooms, hospitals, and doctor offices.

Some 65ers keep Parts A, B, and D, which are government-funded, and opt for a supplemental policy to cover the deductible "gap" rather than sign up for Part C Medicare Advantage.

Medicare kept me healthy enough to stay on the right side of the grass. There was plenty I wanted to accomplish. My wish was to die at home with my boots on, which I did, but I had hoped to have a little warning. Nothing goes as envisioned.

*******

Thankfully, one of my Medicare benefits was a few hours of in-home care services. Moon, the Siberian Forest Cat, was sitting on the counter, wanting some food, when I keeled over. Cheryl, my second-shift caregiver, was in the other room and missed out on all the action. She probably fed Moon before calling 911, which was okay since I wasn't going anywhere.

After I crashed to the floor, dead, and simultaneously began my life again, I wondered if I would save money on health care the next time around. Since I was a kid, I went to the doctor for annual checkups and was treated a few times in the ER for cuts, bruises, and dislocated shoulders.

As time progressed, nuisances such as arthritis and cataracts emerged, along with preventive procedures like colonoscopies and bone density scans. I can't forget all the pharmaceuticals like daily blood pressure, cholesterol pills, and glaucoma-preventing eye drops. Growing up, I took hay fever medicine, codeine-laced cough syrup, and alcohol-infused Ny-Quil.

Then there was all the Metamucil, kale salad, and balanced meals. To what end? Making it to 89 was a good excuse to sit in front of the boob tube. My rationale was that I've never been much of a reader, so I learned story structure ideas and listened to dialogue by watching movies on TV.

*******

"Hey, Siri. Am I dead or alive?" I asked my iPhone helper.

"I'm sorry, but I can't answer that," she replied.

"What good are you?" I lamented as I looked down at all the commotion happening in my kitchen. It wasn't long before the fire engine, ambulance, and police cruiser lights flashed through the front windows. Being reborn old, my arthritic fingers still ached, and my vision was pretty good from the cataract surgery. I presumed I'd start returning to my old self after a few years of growing younger.

The chicken soup wasn't what I would have eaten had I known about my impending death ahead of time. Luckily, I had a habit of eating my "last meals" as often as possible. You know, your requests for food on death row? My last meals are steak and lobster at Svilar's Restaurant in Hudson, Wyoming. I have two eggs over easy, bacon, hashbrowns, and rye toast at Vern's in LaPorte, Colorado. My last lunch would be an Arapaho Taco at the Wind River Casino Willow Room in Riverton, Wyoming.

Cheryl called the guy at the eco-funeral parlor, an obstetrician, and a gerontologist.

I don't know what happened, but during the commotion, someone declared me dead and newly born while the  EMTs and firefighters were coming and going. I hoped Cheryl would use all the leftovers in the fridge, including the cold bowl of chicken noodle soup, for my combination funeral wake/baby shower in the SSV Common House.

I went fast like Mom. I was in good health, except for whatever caused the massive stroke that got me going toward my new life. There was no autopsy, so I'll never know. I hoped I wouldn't die after a lingering disease. My dad had a chronic lung condition that got the best of him. He led a pretty miserable life those last few years.

My business, Boulder Community Media (BCM), was a nonprofit production company. Several years ago, I dissolved BCM and transferred the equipment to the Boulder International Film Festival (BIFF) and the Dairy Center for the Arts.

I had a will and all that. I wasn't as vigilant as I could have been in keeping the list of bank account passwords up to date, but I had to leave my heirs and assigns a few headaches. After I was hosed off and clothed in my usual outfit, cargo shorts and T-shirt, the funeral home crew loaded me onto a gurney. My friends and neighbors set up a long, folding table in the SSV Meditation Room, on which they placed my cardboard coffin, which resembled one of those fold-it-yourself file boxes from Office Depot.

One of my neighbors made a trip to the grocery store to pick up a load of dry ice. That was placed on the bottom of the coffin and covered with a piece of fabric scrounged from the Art Room.

The funeral home crew plopped me into the box and placed more ice between me and the inside of the coffin. My neighbors covered my torso with a woolen maroon Pendleton blanket I picked up at a pawn shop in Lander, Wyoming, to hold in the chill. I spent two days in the Meditation Room. A few familiar people came to mourn my death and rejoice in my birth. Some I didn't recognize. I think they read the birth announcement and my obit in the paper and stopped by to see if there was any free food.

It didn't surprise me that I died and was reborn at 89 after I died. All four of my grandparents were octogenarians. Grandpa Sakata made it to 103. My dad died at 80, but my mom was the outlier at 76. My partner in crime, Diana, ended up moving in with one of her daughters and preceded me in death.

Most of my friends had passed. I had a sister and 21 cousins who were all dead. My sister was childless, but my cousins had kids, and their kids had my second and third cousins. I didn't take the time to get to know many of them. Besides, they were considerably younger and scattered around the world with lives of their own. I didn't expect that any of them would show up. In retrospect, I should have gotten to know at least one of them to be the executor of my estate.

There was a short service in the Common House celebrating my life and rebirth. Cheryl had prepared a good lunch. After everyone cleared out, the funeral parlor guy returned, loaded me up, and delivered me to the tree cemetery.

I was lowered into a vertical hole and was backfilled with a combination of compost and dirt. The guy operating the backhoe planted a tree on top of me and my cardboard coffin.

Then, just like that, I was gone.

Not in pieces, not in pain, but gone. Death had its turn, and I had paid it.

Only I wasn't finished.

# Chapter 2

# Health Scare Crisis: A System in Trouble

I awoke from my dead sleep at the top of the hour on a warm summer day, 17 years earlier in 2025. I breathed a sigh of relief when I saw my iPhone on the coffee table.

"Was that a bad dream? Did I die? I had a dream that Cheryl took my phone!"

The TV in the corner of the room bursts to life with the familiar swirl of music and graphics: *Breaking Tonight: Why America's healthcare costs keep rising.*

As I grew younger, I couldn't help but wonder: What if I could tug at a few threads in the healthcare system fabric that I've lived inside all these years? What if I could change the way this story unfolds, not just for me, but for everyone who finds themselves tethered to a hospital bed with a bar-code on their wrist? I wasn't sure if I wanted to mess with the "Butterfly Effect."

You know, the concept of chaos theory that illustrates how seemingly insignificant actions or events can lead to large, unpredictable consequences over time. The term comes from the metaphorical idea that the flap of a butterfly's wings in one part of the world could set off a chain of atmospheric events that eventually influences the path of a tornado elsewhere. Small things matter, and the cause-and-effect relationships in complex systems, like my life, are nonlinear and unpredictable.

"Mergers and acquisitions are reshaping the healthcare landscape," The anchor on the TV leaned forward. "A new synergy."

Synergy? I say monopoly. What if my younger self had spoken louder at local protests, in letters to the editor, in conversations with neighbors? I couldn't change the outcomes of healthcare consolidation, but it was frustrating.

The pundits interpret graphs and percentages, but what I have experienced is more complicated. On the one hand, I'm shocked that KP priced a simple medical check-up like a luxury vacation, with medicine that costs more than my HOA payment, listed on a "this is not a bill" report with a dozen line items that might as well be in cosmic top-secret code.

State regulators established measures regarding price transparency, but the ambulance driver and my bedside nurse didn't give me any options because events moved so quickly in an emergency situation. Maybe my service providers did tell me, but I was too out of it to recall. I was surprised at some of the services that my insurance didn't cover. I could have used more advocacy.

Beneath the frustration, I'm grateful. Because if I had been born just a generation earlier, I might not have survived long enough to complain. The very innovations that inflate today's balance sheets also saved me. The machines that could peer inside my chest, the drugs that could steady my heartbeat, and the surgeries that once would have been impossible were expensive. Then KP filed for reimbursement from Medicare for the exorbitant cost. I might be healthier, but I feel for young people. Who knows what healthcare costs will be when they are eligible for Medicare? That age has been steadily rising.

That's the paradox: equal parts outrage and thankfulness. Profit motive has crippled the system, but the miracles are real.

I know the bullet points by heart. High prices. Administrative complexity. Pharmaceuticals. Consolidation.

Here in my new present, I wonder: as I grow younger, maybe there's something I can do besides sigh at the bills and shake my head at the TV. Perhaps I can teach my younger self to ask questions in real-time.

I could have joined those early pushes for price transparency, even if they seemed quixotic at the time. I could have viewed every confusing Explanation of Benefits not just as a personal headache but as a breadcrumb trail leading to a bigger truth.

I lived through the COVID-19 pandemic in chaos, but as I grow younger, I'll remember my old age as a big lesson and not wait for a crisis like that to fester. This time around, I'll tell my younger self to pay more attention to prevention, to the small habits and community investments that keep diseases from becoming catastrophes.

Seeing those graphics on TV reminded me of the gadgets that dazzled me and drained my bank account and credit cards when I was on my deathbed. As I step backward through time, I can carry with me the reminder that technology is only as humane as the way it's used. Maybe I could have asked harder questions about who benefited: the patient, or the shareholders behind the shiny new equipment or pharmaceutical?

One talking head mentioned labor shortages. I saw nurses sprinting, and the doctors seemed to age overnight. As I grow younger, I'll channel some of my frustration and advocate for safe staffing ratios, or at least offering gratitude while it still matters. I did the best I could and stood in solidarity when healthcare workers went on strike.

The experts finish their debate. The graphics faded. I'm still here, with the uneasy thought that being a patient didn't mean I was powerless.

The news reminded me that the system is vast, tangled, and often indifferent. Yet as I grow older, perhaps I can choose to remember that every system is also built on choices made by administrators, insurers, politicians, and, yes, by patients who either speak up or stay silent.

I can't stop mergers between big businesses, nor could I have rewritten the pricing codes or fixed the labor shortages. Maybe I could have changed outcomes in smaller ways by writing one more letter, making one more call, showing up to one more meeting, refusing to shrug when someone told me, "That's just the way it is."

My TV screen faded to black. I imagined my younger self watching the same news with sharper ears, stronger lungs, and more stubborn hope.

*******

Then the TV picture faded up. An advertisement appeared for a weight-loss regimen called Noom, a health and wellness program designed to help individuals achieve their weight loss goals. I wasn't obese by any stretch of the imagination, but over the years, I've known people who were on some diet all the time. Why couldn't they keep off the weight?

Based on recent data, the Centers for Disease Control and Prevention (CDC) reported that from 2021 to 2023, the age-adjusted prevalence of obesity among U.S. adults was 40.3 percent. This is a significant increase from previous decades, when the rate was around 30.5 percent in 2000.

On the other hand, separate and overlapping industries.

Weight loss programs like Noom are a part of the business paradox. On the one hand, the food industry, particularly companies that produce highly processed, calorie-dense foods and beverages, profits from the widespread consumption of their products. These products are often cheaper and more convenient, making them a cornerstone of many people's diets. In contrast, others sell everything from supplements to gym memberships and profit directly from people's desire to lose weight. On the other hand, some of the same food conglomerates that sell high-calorie foods also own brands of "diet" or "healthy" foods.

The pharmaceutical and healthcare industrial complex addresses the health consequences of obesity. There is a growing market for anti-obesity medications and over-the-counter drugs for related conditions, such as diabetes and heart disease, which represents a significant source of revenue for pharmaceutical companies.

In turn, the burden of obesity on the healthcare system is immense, with medical costs related to obesity in the U.S. reaching billions of dollars annually. Hospitals, doctors, and other healthcare providers are all part of a system that treats the diseases and conditions associated with obesity.

Obesity is not only a public health crisis, but also a profitable business model. The system is designed to create and then solve the problem, with various industries benefiting at different stages.

I've been a part of this conundrum since I was on my high school wrestling team. I developed the discipline to lose weight quickly. That habit followed me through life, and if I wanted to shed a few pounds, I followed the Atkins Diet. My regimen consisted of fasting for two days, followed by a period of cutting out carbohydrates. I was a voracious omnivore, so mainly eating meat and vegetables went well with my favorite foods.

The Atkins is a low-carbohydrate diet developed by Dr. Robert Atkins. It emphasizes protein, fat, and vegetables while limiting carbohydrates. The goal of the diet is to burn fat rather than carbohydrates for energy. The Atkins Diet has been popular since the early 2000s, although I had practiced the concepts well before then. Proponents of the Atkins Diet claim that it provides numerous health benefits, including weight loss and improved blood sugar control. Opponents say the diet increases cholesterol, causes indigestion, bad breath, and makes it difficult to maintain weight loss.

Even in old age, I had a five-pound beer belly that I could stand to shed, so I signed up for the seven-day free trial to explore the combined personalized meal plan, goal-setting, food tracking, and behavior-change coaching to eat more strategically.

The Noom approach wasn't new to me. One of the basic tenets is "progress is better than perfection." This time, going through life in reverse, I'll continue to be thoughtful about my food choices, but splurge less on potato chips and caramel popcorn. Maybe next time, I'll last until I'm 92.

One Noom lesson was about snacking. I chased the high-calorie dinner I prepared with eight grapes and a Clementine orange. In the morning, if I didn't skip it, my breakfast of choice, even before Noom, was a hard-boiled egg or leftovers. I often missed lunch in favor of a snack before a big dinner. My doctors always questioned why, on some days, I only had one meal. "That's not healthy," they said. "Drink more water," they said.

I did lose a few pounds, but as it turned out, it didn't matter. As I grow younger, I cringe every time I see a weight loss drug ad on TV, followed by a news segment about a celebrity preparing their greasiest BBQ steak.

Unseen powers handed a second chance, and if I do get a little chubby, I'll lapse back to my low-carb, high-protein food regimen. My body still carried the scars of my first life, and eight loss measures being the least of them compared to the daily reality of arthritis grinding my joints or the constant burn of post-herpetic neuralgia (PHN).

For all the triumphs of modern medicine, the machines that restart hearts, the drugs that fight infections, pain remains a puzzle Western doctors can't seem to solve.

I expected the white-coated experts to have answers. Instead, I found them baffled, shrugging at my pain symptoms, and offering little more than pills that dulled my mind without easing my body. That's when I realized that the next chapter of my journey wasn't only about the healthcare system keeping me alive, but about learning to live with suffering that medicine doesn't yet understand, like my chronic pain.

# Chapter 3

# Chronic Pain: High Tech Solutions

When I got the pains of death out of the way and was alive again, I still resided at Silver Sage Village and relied on my memories as filters through which I viewed my new and different life. Even though I was younger in an old body, my chronic pain hadn't improved, and I've been dealing with it.

My Western doctors shrugged and said there wasn't much that they could do. I refused to give up. Pain had planted itself in my life, but I wasn't going to let it take over like a weed patch. So I went looking for other ways.

I tried acupuncture, which is supposed to balance the body's energy, or *qi*, and improve circulation. Sometimes those tiny needles felt like a reset button, as if someone had untangled a knot deep inside me. Other times, the relief was subtle, like a whisper. It helped enough to keep me coming back.

Then came yoga. At first, I couldn't stretch far or hold the poses, but I learned that wasn't the point. Yoga wasn't about touching my toes, but was about quieting my mind and softening the edges of the pain. With every slow stretch and breath, I carved out a little space between me and the ache.

I heard about Cognitive Behavioral Therapy for chronic pain (CBT) on one of the Sunday morning TV shows. It's a skills-based treatment that helps people manage pain by changing unhelpful thoughts and behaviors and addressing how emotions, thoughts, and actions interact to intensify pain.

I've been adapting CBT by integrating the effects from acupuncture needles, yoga stretches, and training my mind to reshape my pain. Pain isn't only physical. Our thoughts, emotions, and behaviors can amplify it. If we retrain them, they can help turn down the volume.

The TV doctor explained that pain is like a fire alarm that keeps blaring, even when the house isn't on fire. CBT doesn't rip the alarm off the wall. It helps you learn to quiet it, to keep it from taking over your whole life. In practice, this meant being aware of my thought patterns.

When I thought, "The pain will never go away, I can't stand this," that didn't add to my healing.

"I've handled this before, and I have tools to manage it now," was my thought that replaced my negative belief with something positive.

CBT gave me another option to supplement what I've been doing to keep pain from controlling every moment of my day. Alongside acupuncture and yoga, it became part of my patchwork approach to live alongside chronic pain without letting it define me.

This integrated approach made me think about how complex my chronic pain had become. Even though I was getting younger, the pain made my life more complicated, as I had to balance it with my day-to-day activities. Based on my perceptions of technology, by the 21st century, I expected every family to drive flying cars and have a robotic housekeeper like Rosey on the 1960s TV show, *The Jetsons*. Rosey prepared meals, babysat young Elroy, and offered dating advice to teenager Judy.

Gadgets from the future haven't become a place, but when I awoke from my dead sleep, I still envisioned robots like Rosey would be there to help me out and provide companionship, particularly as an aged adult. Those innovations made for good headlines. Robot prototypes haven't come close to being practical realities. They're pricey and too complicated for everyday use.

*******

I wondered if, in 2025, there were any accessible, affordable tools that I could adapt to make my daily life easier. My chronic pain had compounded. Dealing with the constant pain was getting on my nerves.

What could I do about it?

For many older adults, as well as their family members and caregivers, the simplest technologies are already within reach, sitting on a nightstand or in a pocket. Lucky for me, I was getting younger, but in the meantime, I had to take a few steps to make dealing with pain easier by reducing the stress caused by forgetfulness and having to juggle my life in a fast-paced world.

**-Smart Speakers:** I recently programmed my Amazon Alexa device to remind me to take my medication first thing in the morning and to check my Google Calendar. It's a simple feature, but one that brings peace of mind.

There are other similar devices on the market, but Alexa seems to be the most flexible and user-friendly for this kind of purpose. With a few voice commands, it can become a reliable daily companion.

**-Smartphones:** I still had PHN, a chronic pain condition that has resisted every treatment I've tried. After I watched the TV program segment about CBT. I created shortcuts on my iPhone to help me by sending me text message prompts every couple of hours.

"You're healthy. Think of positive images and experiences" is an example. These nudges have reminded me to take back some control over my day and my mindset. A caregiver or relative could easily set up similar prompts for an older loved one, whether as CBT-CP, for encouragement, reminders, or even for a touch of companionship.

**–AirTags:** This doesn't have anything to do with chronic pain, but there's also the question of safety. As a member of the Boulder Police Oversight Panel, I once joined a patrol where officers spent two hours searching for a woman with memory issues who had wandered from home. Eventually, a family member found her in a neighborhood far from where we had been searching.

This experience made me think about Apple AirTags and similar tracking devices. I used one to keep tabs on my luggage on a vacation cruise to the Bahamas. My bags were lost, but I tracked the AirTag and was relieved to know that my suitcase was on the ship. Imagine if a caregiver outfitted a person prone to wandering with such a tag. The reassurance for family members and caregivers would be enormous, giving them confidence and saving critical time in emergencies.

**–AI Chatbots:** Beyond smart speakers and smartphone shortcuts, Artificial Intelligence conversational chatbots offered me a new level of personalized support. You've probably had a chat bubble pop up when you're figuring out how to enter your healthcare portal or are unable to locate your monthly statements on your bank's website.

I trained a conversational chatbot called Alan-Bot with specific information about my health records and prescriptions. I also uploaded prompts to reinforce my CBT reminders from Alexa and Siri. Users can adapt the same technology, while still in its infancy, with specific, individualized information about a person.

"Your granddaughter Harper loves painting." If someone struggles to recall relatives, the caregiver can feed short bios and stories into the chatbot to prompt recognition.

"The oval yellowish pill is Protonix, which controls your stomach acid, and is taken orally once a day before breakfast." Alan-Bot provided me with clear, step-by-step instructions about medications.

I accessed Alan-Bot through a free app on my iPhone, which made setup straightforward.

Family members or caregivers can create a user profile, feed in relevant information, and update it as needed. Looking ahead, AI could make a digital companion that blends practical support with gentle companionship, expanding to include story-sharing, adaptive reminders, and safety prompts.

*******

Of course, no technology can replace human companionship. The most effective way to close the loneliness gap will always be through person-to-person interaction, such as visits from family, chats with neighbors, and phone calls from friends. Technology can play a vital supporting role, creating more opportunities for connection, reducing stress for caregivers, and giving older adults tools to feel more independent and secure.

The SSV's underlying philosophy emphasized human interactions, from maintaining the property together to socializing at community dinners. The resident average age has increased to 74, compared to 18 years earlier, when it was in the 60s.

Cohousing is a hedge against loneliness, but as we've continued to help each other out, personal needs increase and interactions decrease. Neighbors spend more time away, as we get the most out of the twilight of our lives.

Instead of seeing technology as a substitute for community, I've used it as a bridge that blends digital innovation with human compassion, keeping us all closer, safer, and less alone. My SSV neighbors were there once again for support after another emergency surgery, which added yet another source of pain to my chronic condition in 2023 when my dream vacation turned into a nightmare.

# Chapter 4

# Cruise to Panama: Surgery Abroad

When December 31, 2023, came around, I was anxiously waiting around home. Kaiser Permanente had electronically transferred $29,200 and change into my bank account, just in time for me to pay off all my maxed-out credit cards. It felt like a strange kind of Christmas bonus, though it was really a reimbursement for medical expenses. The money arrived exactly a month after I had spent two long weeks in the Punta Pacifica Hospital in Panama City. That emergency surgery was the inciting incident for another healthcare scare, five years after the previous one. Close calls generally happened to me around every 20 years.

Time was speeding up for me.

I didn't imagine I'd be comparing hospital bills like postcards from my travels. I marveled that 10 days, which included the surgery, recovery, food, nurses, doctors, and the extra attention at the Panama City hospital, added up to $29,200. It was a bargain, though it didn't feel like bargain care. I had attentive doctors, more nurses than I could count, and staff who never seemed hurried or too busy to notice me.

Compare that to what happened a week earlier, when I was back home in Boulder. A flare of pain landed me in Boulder

Community Hospital with a diagnosis of an esophageal ulcer. Three days, no surgery, and my bill was $29,000.

On paper, it was upside down. Ten days in Panama with surgery was cheaper than three days in Colorado without going under the knife? In my gut, it didn't seem right. The care in Panama wasn't just "good enough," it was better with more hands on deck, more time, and more humanity.

Of course, I was aware of the reasons. In Panama, the cost of living is lower. Nurses and doctors don't command the same salaries they do in the U.S. The price of medicine, bandages, and hospital meals is all a fraction of what they cost in Boulder. Hospitals there don't need to staff armies of billing clerks just to navigate the maze of insurance codes. Malpractice insurance doesn't hover like a storm cloud over every decision. The system is simpler, leaner, and more affordable.

My gastroenterologist instructed me to schedule an appointment with Dr. Lookner.

Out-of-country emergency surgery must be common. Dr. Lookner said three of his patients had undergone unforeseen procedures overseas. KP has an uncomplicated reimbursement claim request form that I filled out. I was hopeful that KP would cover most of my expenses. I also had travel insurance that would cover any co-pay gap, reimburse me for lost days at sea, and my transportation from Panama City to Colorado.

"Your endoscopic results indicate you have an early-stage esophageal ulcer. Barrett's esophagus," he explained. "Stomach acid had eaten away at the lining of your lower esophagus. The constant irritation could have been happening for years and has a higher risk of transforming into esophageal adenocarcinoma."

Cancer, just what I needed to worry about on top of my chronic pain.

Dr. Lookner, like my Panamanian doctor, prescribed a bland diet, no caffeine, and to eat small portions.

*******

How did I end up in the hospital? After I returned to Boulder from Panama City, the pain after my abdominal surgery hadn't let up. It got worse, considering it compounded my existing pain. By Christmas Eve, my stools had turned black, and I had developed a cough that compounded my strange poops.

Diana and I were planning to go to her daughter Amanda's house on Christmas Eve. Both conditions had worsened. I summoned my next-door neighbor, Henry, to give me a ride to the hospital on Christmas Eve morning. SSV has a mutual aid group that provides resident transportation for almost any reason, with no questions asked.

"Let's go to Boulder Community Hospital," Henry suggested. "We should go to the closest emergency department."

"My hospital is Good Samaritan in Lafayette," I told him.

"The state passed a new law. Anyone can go to any emergency room and stay over if they need to, just not too long. Remember when you drove me here before, when I had those chest pains? Same deal," Henry explained.

We pulled up in the drop-off area. I was the only one in the lobby and was admitted on the spot, not knowing that my heart rate was 130 and my blood pressure was very low. After being rehydrated by an IV, the ER doctor admitted me for bacterial pneumonia.

"If you are on regular insurance, it's not like Medicare," my case manager said. "You could be kicked out after one day, if not sooner. I'm sorry you'll have to spend Christmas with us."

"It's not the first time," I explained. "My holidays have been different since my parents died in 2003. "You Can't Always Get What You Want," as Mick Jagger says."

I wasn't feeling that great. Diana and Amanda stopped by on Christmas morning just in time for the main event. I felt nauseous and barfed up black vomit. Amanda summoned Dr. Google. Coffee ground vomit was a sign of blood leaking into my upper gastrointestinal tract.

The morning after Christmas, I went into surgery for an Esophago-Gastro-Duodenoscopy (EGD) test. The procedure uses an endoscope to examine the lining of the esophagus, stomach, and first part of the small intestine. I was under full anesthesia, but beforehand, the doctor explained that he would be guiding a lighted tube with a camera at the end. He removed some tissue samples and had them sent to a pathology lab for analysis.

*******

Once again, I found myself caught in the familiar cycle: pain, hospitals, tests, recovery, punctuated with the financial stress of trying to stay afloat while my body kept pulling me under.

The hospitalist released me a day after my procedure. I don't think there was much more he could have done for me. I'm thinking that three days was the limit for a hospital stay. My case manager said that I could appeal my release if I felt I needed more time under the hospital's care.

No thanks.

Ten days before, I was released from the hospital in Panama City. I stayed over at a nearby Marriott before flying out the next morning. A snowstorm nearly kept me from landing. I was dressed for the tropics and didn't have much of a winter wardrobe, as I had packed light for the cruise. I managed to layer two T-shirts, a hoodie, and pulled on a pair of socks to go with my Keens.

I cleared customs and rode the RTD airport bus to Boulder. Diana and our neighbor, Lindy, met me at the Walnut Street Station in Downtown Boulder.

"Everyone will want to hear how you're doing," Lindy said while loading my bag into the back of her Subaru. "The holiday potluck and White Elephant gift exchange is tonight."

"My doctor said I should take it easy and not overdo the eating."

"The new guy is roasting a turkey," Diana said. "I wrote us down for mashed potatoes."

"It'll be a good time to try out my new diet. The potatoes will be perfect." I wasn't too crazy about eating anything.

The meal was pretty good. I took tiny portions of turkey, potatoes, and peas, which I mixed together. We are all good about clearing the table and loading the dishwasher before the gift exchange.

One of my upstairs neighbors, Dan, went to the tree and fetched a small package, and opened it up to find an overnight kit from the Pacifica Salud Hospital.

"It was too late for me to figure out anything else to contribute," I said. "It was my souvenir from Panama."

"You were in the hospital for a long time. What happened?" asked Dan.

"We were on a 15-day cruise from LA to Miami via the Panama Canal. Luckily, the ship was in port at Panama City when I got sick. I had a restless night and vomited up my French onion soup and pepperoni pizza. The next morning, I felt better but sensed something wasn't right and stumbled to the ship's medical center. It was closed.

The sign said to call 911. Someone inside answered. I made my condition sound worse than it was so that the attendant would answer the door. I was let in and was there all afternoon. After an X-ray showed an intestinal blockage, I was taken off the ship and transported by ambulance to the Punta Pacifica Hospital."

*******

The ambulance rambled through Panama City. Occasionally, the lights and sirens would blare through busy intersections. A nurse met me at the ship's emergency room, where a doctor examined me.

Before my treatment was too far along, a woman from the business office asked for $2,700 prepayment for emergency services. I paid by credit card. I was soon admitted and met the hospitalist, Dr. Ruben Urena. He was an English speaker and the liaison with the Norwegian Cruise Line.

"I ordered a CAT scan for the morning," the doctor said. "We'll hook you up to an IV to rehydrate you. Your white blood cell count was high, and we'll add a painkiller and some antibiotics." A nurse stuck a Nasogastric (NG) tube up my nose and into my stomach to remove fluids and gas to relieve pain and pressure. "This could be a partial blockage and will improve on its own. Most bowel obstructions are partial blockages," the doctor optimistically advised.

Soon after a nurse helped me settle into room 729, the business office made another visit. I had to prepay $7,000 before the surgery. Nobody spoke English. Everyone used Google Translate. I like immersing myself in local communities. My *espanglish* began to come back.

After the finance office approved my payment, the gastrointestinal surgeon, Dr. Varga, wanted me to wait a day to see if the NG tube would alleviate the blockage. I insisted that he perform the surgery immediately. The hospital staff got me ready and wheeled me downstairs around 8:30 p.m. I remember seeing a yellow mask placed over my nose, and then I woke up an hour later.

*******

The following morning, Dr. Varga reported that my decision to have the surgery sooner was a good one. My stomach contents had turned darker, which was "muy mal" (very bad).

I slept pretty well. A nurse hooked me up to a bag of *alimento* nutrient solution since I couldn't eat. The care was excellent. The nursing staff woke me up at all hours to take my blood pressure and draw blood. Sometimes, I woke up, but most times, I was dead to the world.

The hospital provided internet service. I could make myself understood, but there were medical terms that I didn't know, such as *dolor*, meaning "pain," and *hinchado*, meaning "swelling."

The finance office runner visited me again and asked that I pay $9,000 for the post-operative recovery.

A few days later, a nurse removed the *alimento* bag. Dr. Urena cleared me to follow a clear liquid diet, consisting of Jell-O, tea, and soup. When I farted, the dietician switched me to solid food. I liked the fresh fruit, which included small bananas that are tastier and sweeter than large ones, as well as papaya. By the time the meals reached the 7th floor, the heavy food, such as chicken or beef covered in gravy, had cooled. I wished that my appetite were better, because the food looked and smelled good.

Diana had stayed on the ship and completed the cruise through the Panama Canal to Cartagena, Colombia, and Miami before returning to Boulder. When she checked out, the purser charged $3,000 to my credit card for my time in the onboard medical center.

*******

On December 8, 2023, a polite young man from the business office visited me with my final bill. I owed another $7,500 that I had to pay before I was released. I was passing gas, and there wasn't much more the hospital could do for me, and Dr. Urena kicked me out. I walked two blocks to the Marriott Hotel, which anchored a large shopping mall, where I spent the night before flying nonstop from Panama City to Denver.

I've wondered what it would be like to be far away from home with a major medical issue, which wasn't a surprise. My biggest "aha" moment was experiencing what it would be like to have no insurance. I don't know what I would have done had my credit lines run out. I didn't bother to ask, but I imagine the hospital would have offered me a high-interest financing plan.

In the United States, a financial gravitational force influences hospital prices. Hospitals price every pill, every IV bag, and every minute in a bed, as though I were underwriting the whole system, including research, overhead, cross-subsidies, and the inevitable piles of paperwork. That gravity means the per-day price in the Boulder hospital is nearly four times higher than in Panama City.

No one books a ticket to America for cut-rate healthcare. The irony is that while the U.S. exports medical breakthroughs, uninsured Americans can't afford to buy them. Panama, on the other hand, positions itself as a haven for those of us willing to travel for competent, compassionate, and affordable care.

It shouldn't take an international flight to remind me that healing isn't supposed to lead me into bankruptcy.

*******

"That's quite a story," Dan said before getting up to check out the dessert table.

"You can give out my hospital shampoo kit at next year's White Elephant gift exchange."

That was a good thing about living at Silver Sage Village. Some rituals are predictable.

# Chapter 5

# Silver Sage Village:
# Senior Cohousing

Silver Sage Village wasn't exactly an old folks' home, but all the residents were 50 and older. Members provide support to one another, which is the foundation of cohousing communities, similar to the Baby Boomer neighborhoods of the 1960s. When it comes to providing personal care, like wiping a neighbor's butt, it's time to move out.

At SSV, people live in private dwellings. They have agreed to share in the operation of the community as a Homeowners Association (HOA) and participate in maintaining common spaces, such as the courtyard garden. In the case of SSV, the owners agreed on a set of values by which to live. Approximately 30 of us meet monthly and make decisions through a consensus process. Contrast that with a regular HOA.

The owners meet yearly to elect a Board of Directors that makes all the decisions. At the time, there were five cohousing communities in Boulder, including Nomad Cohousing, where I would later meet a woman from Houston, Texas, named Cherie, who established her residency in Boulder.

I moved my business, Boulder Community Media (BCM), to an empty office at SSV. That's been handy. Moving out of

Downtown Boulder was a tough decision, but necessary. The landlord evicted all the tenants from the building.

Initially, I experienced downtown withdrawal because my space was located in the heart of the Pearl Street Mall, within walking distance of numerous bars, restaurants, and other activities. BCM produced multiple TV programs based on music events, art shows, and unique individuals wandering around the Mall.

The move was a good excuse to downsize, though. I sorted through outdated video cameras, cables, and miscellaneous equipment and hauled the detritus to the secondhand store. There was plenty of room in my new office for the necessary production equipment and an editing station.

The SSV Common House was perfect and offered similar amenities to those I had downtown. There was a TV room for screening, two private spaces for interviews, and a large commercial kitchen to entertain friends and colleagues.

I had settled into a routine. Walking from my condo to my office, just 20 feet away, at 4:30 a.m., was a great way to start the day. Moving into the SSV senior community was a good place to begin anew, mainly since I was un-aging and relatively free of aches and pains. Even though I was no longer decrepit and getting younger every day, it was good to know there would be neighbors around.

*******

Diana and I were lucky to find SSV. I was a budding creative entrepreneur in 2010, and Diana was retired but working part-time. We qualified for the city of Boulder's Affordable Housing Program and were able to purchase a home from the lower-cost inventory. Just when two people and two dogs were on their last legs, we learned that a guy had died at SSV in the next block.

The late fellow's heirs had a tough time selling the place because it was an "affordable" unit in a cohousing community. Not only did prospective buyers need to be income-qualified, but they would also want to live and collaborate with a bunch of other older people. I knew the SSV developer, Jim, from my stint on the city of Boulder Planning Board. Ironically, he presented the SSV project to the board many years earlier.

In the dead of a wintry December, Henry Kroll, the guy who drove me to the hospital from time to time, would be my eventual neighbor, trudging through the snow wearing a goofy hat. He was serving wine and passing out business cards.

"Come and visit Silver Sage Village," he said as he filled a paper cup with cabernet. "We're one block that way." Henry pointed toward the East. Jim invited us to look at the condo that met all our criteria. The unit was 800 square feet and had two bedrooms, which is larger than our townhouse in Studio Mews. The other issue was selling it, which had been on the market since the summer, a time when it should have been an excellent opportunity to sell. On top of the lagging market during the housing crisis, our realtor and neighbor unexpectedly took his life.

It turned out that Diana learned from a young mom dropping off her kid at the preschool where she worked that her mother wanted to move to Boulder and needed a place to live. Shortly after we relisted the townhouse, she bought our condo, and we relocated 600 feet down the street into SSV.

I understood cohousing as an intellectual matter. I knew there was a high level of consensus-building among the neighbors, which meant lots of meetings. Each resident was expected to join one or two teams responsible for various aspects of operation and maintenance. I was also aware that there were potluck meals twice a week. I joined the "Community Development" team that organized parties. Other groups handled the finances, maintained the Common House, and tended to the garden.

The community members shared potluck dinners twice a week. Invariably, the conversations more often than not circled around to aging and medical concerns.

One meal, I lamented about my dentist appointment that day. My insurance covered two basic teeth cleanings. I required three deep periodontal cleanings three times a year. The third dental grinding, picking, and buffing was an unnecessary out-of-pocket expense. Then I read a fascinating book that changed my outlook on my mouth and nose.

Chapter 6

# Mouth Taping: Clean Straight Teeth

A friend of mine recommended a book to me that she claimed would change my life. I had bad teeth, which I had inherited from Dad's side of the family. I brushed and flossed regularly, likely more often than the average person.

For as long as I could remember, I woke up in the early hours with a dry mouth, gasping for air. I heard about a book called *Breath: The New Science of a Lost Art* by James Nestor. Nestor's main point is that modern humans breathe through their mouth instead of their noses. He attributes chronic illnesses like asthma, anxiety, attention deficit hyperactivity disorder, psoriasis, and others to mouth breathing. Nose breathing could improve those conditions.

According to Nestor, today's human breathing problems began when people learned to cook and speak. Subsistence farming became commercialized, allowing for the mass production of softer, prepared foods that could be readily available to feed workers, thereby fueling the Industrial Revolution. Less time spent eating resulted in greater productivity, but an unintended consequence was that human faces became weakened from underuse due to less chewing and more swallowing.

Nestor writes that the prehistoric hominids who came before *homo sapiens* 1.5 million years ago learned to cut up their food and harness fire. Over time, the efficient use of food meant higher caloric intake and larger brains. More brains meant our sinus cavities became smaller, and our protruding noses became narrower. Humans developed better survival instincts.

The increased brain capacity led to the development of human speech. Nestor says that as our voices evolved, so did the need for our mouths to create different sounds, resulting in smaller lips and a deeper larynx in the throat. The downside to articulating words was a susceptibility to choking on food.

My modern mouth with poor airflow and nasal congestion meant that I inhaled air inefficiently through my mouth. I didn't need to go to the extent Nestor did to prove the point. He plugged both nostrils to simulate congestion for two weeks while monitoring his vital signs regularly.

Soon after he began the experiment, Nestor's blood pressure had increased to the first stage of hypertension, his pulse increased, and his body temperature dropped. His snoring worsened while his oxygen levels fell below 90 percent.

As human mouths became smaller, teeth were crowded and crooked. Such was the case with me. My teeth have always been one of my physical weak points. Since I was young, I've had to schedule teeth cleaning and examinations on a trimester basis rather than twice a year. As an adult in Boulder, I've always gone to corporate dentists because of the ease of scheduling, and there are Comfort Dental offices all over the place, including one within walking distance of SSV.

My dentists, and I've had a lot of them peeking down my throat, have all pointed out that my crooked bottom teeth were problematic due to excessive plaque buildup. They chart my periodontal health by poking around my gums. Many readings were 3 to 5 mm, meaning the tissue surrounding my teeth was deteriorating. Even though I flossed and brushed regularly, that wasn't enough. My gums required remediation, and one dentist referred me to a periodontist. Another friend recounted her experience with the oral surgery. Based on that, I didn't want anything to do with that pain.

*******

I was watching TV one afternoon in September 2019. A commercial for SmileDirectClub (Smile) featured form-fitting plastic aligners that patients periodically changed to straighten their teeth. One of my now estranged friends described oral skin grafts and the pain involved with her periodontal surgery. Based on that vivid description, I didn't want to see a periodontist as my dentist suggested.

Before the Smile commercial was over, I dialed the 1-800 number on the screen and asked if there was an office in Boulder, which there was. The following day, I made an appointment at the 15th Street office two blocks from the Network Family Wellness Center. An administrative person who doubled as the dental assistant greeted me. She helped me fill out the paperwork and arrange for payment. At that time, the price was $1,600.00 for the aligners. The next step was to take pictures of my teeth. Rather than X-rays, the Smile assistant scanned the inside of my mouth with a digital movie camera.

I remembered my childhood. I must have been in the 7th grade when my orthodontist, Dr. Gorny, applied regular stainless steel braces to my teeth during junior high school. Nestor says that Dr. Gorny's traditional brand of orthodontics contributed to my small mouth and subsequent breathing problem.

I was a generation too late and could have benefited from "functional orthodontic" practices, including Twin Block devices introduced in the 1980s. Two "blocks" fit over the upper and lower teeth. The upper block was connected to the lower block by a wire or elastic band, which gently moved the jaw into its proper position.

A Twin Block appliance would have addressed my bite and jaw alignment issues by strengthening my facial muscles and repositioning my jaw, rather than just moving my teeth into the gap created when my dentist, Dr. Carson, removed one of my lower incisors.

The Office Manager sent off my scans to a Smile facility. A few weeks later, I received enough incrementally different form-fitting aligners to last two years. I was surprised by how tightly the first one fit, but it was not as painful as the braces installed by my orthodontist when I was in junior high school.

The kit came with pieces of foam that, when I bit down on them, seated the aligner that immediately began shifting my teeth. The instruction was to wear them all the time, except when eating or drinking.

I completed the program and was amazed at the results, which were strictly cosmetic and did nothing to enlarge my mouth or airway. When I went for my dental check-up, the dentist complimented me on how my oral hygiene had reduced the plaque buildup. I explained it was due to my straighter teeth, but my gums were still not as healthy as they could be.

I followed Nestor's advice and, during the day, consciously breathed through my nose. I bought a box of one-inch breathable plastic surgical tape and sealed my mouth shut with an inch of tape at night. When I had to clear my throat or cough while asleep, the gaps on either side of my mouth allowed the air to flow. When I needed a sip of water, I unfastened the tape on my top lip. Nestor says that nose breathing strengthens my airways and regulates my metabolism.

My dreams were also more vivid.

The next time I had my teeth cleaned was after I started taping my mouth closed. My dentist mentioned that my dental hygiene had improved due to my straighter teeth and mouth, which remained moist throughout the night. My improved gum measurements were 1 to 3 mm. I was no longer scared awake by loud snoring or gasping. That led to restful sleep, but the most significant financial benefit was one less dental cleaning per year.

Mouth taping was a simple fix that saved me money and lowered my nocturnal stress. I was still not as flexible as I once was and still had to deal with occasional nuisance injuries. Nestor's book provided me with insight into the importance of integrated health practices, which led me to a unique chiropractor.

Chapter 7

# Network: Pain in the Back

I'd been leading a very sedentary life and became more active as I grew younger. I didn't get much out and was content to sit in front of my computer and work on my writing projects. I'd never been much of a reader. Nestor's book is the first one I'd completed in ages. I learned about story structure and analyzed content while watching TV and listening to dialogue. I admit that most times I tried to watch something on TV at 8:00 p.m., I dozed off before the end and had to revisit the program or movie "on demand."

My early morning writing schedule went uninterrupted until I developed lower back pain, which was a nuisance but severe enough to occasionally wake me up at night.

When I was a sophomore in high school, I had a sports injury that threw out my back. My dad had a similar problem, and he took me to see his chiropractor, who popped and snapped my bones into place.

While sitting in front of my computer or TV, I felt the same dull ache I had when I was 16 years old. My Apple wristwatch would buzz me with reminders that it was time to stand, and I'd take a break and walk around. I was still driving for five or six hours at a time to movie production locations. I could barely make it to Cheyenne, 90 minutes away, without having to stop in Fort Collins for a stretch break.

I didn't want to overdose on Advil and bought one of those lower-back massage devices with heat from Bed Bath & Beyond that plugged into a standard home outlet and my car battery. That worked, but was only remedial. Diana was on the Network Family Wellness Center (Network) email list and received periodic invitations to a free dinner at a local Mexican restaurant. Network acquires new patients by providing food in exchange for listening to a service pitch.

After dinner, Dr. Danny Knowles made a presentation about his spinal care practice, a holistic approach to healing the spine and nervous system that improves overall health and quality of life through self-healing. The deal was a free-of-charge, no-obligation evaluation. Depending on the result, I could take it or leave it. My lower back pain was irritating enough that I signed up for a year and made an appointment.

It turned out that the same curved spine I had been diagnosed with as a teenager contributed to my current aches and pains. The primary difference between Network and traditional chiropractic treatments is that there is no twisting of bones or neck popping. The practice is communal, with four patients treated concurrently. I'm not sure if this was the case, but I felt that the collective energy contributed to my overall wellness. Including waiting time, the drop-in treatments took anywhere from 30 minutes to an hour.

The concept behind Network was a mystery to me. In addition to the periodic treatments, Network offered workshops. One was a demonstration with explanations about Network treatment outcomes. One of the chiropractors had severe scoliosis (spine curvature). She was face down on the table, and the doctor performed his healing touches. I observed her spine undulating under her shirt like a snake side-winding its way under a piece of fabric. That was one of the strangest things I've seen.

"Very precise and gentle physical force applications are applied to the spine and surrounding regions, initiating a reorganizational process resulting in a readjustment of the affected nerve and spinal tissue," is the explanation given on the website. "This results from respiration increasing in the sacral pelvic region, up the mid-back, and through a person's neck. This is known as the respiratory wave and is the first healing wave. Simultaneously, a second healing wave known as the somatopsychic (body-mind) wave is coordinated by the brain and travels along the spine and through the extremities and central nervous system, promoting the development of new health and wellness strategies."

When I began treatments, I couldn't feel the respiratory or somatopsychic waves I saw during the workshop. My back pain went away after my second visit. It could have been natural healing, but Network helped alleviate my lower back pain and improved my overall wellness.

Network treatments were a subscription service and varied from patient to patient. The initial check-up involved spinal X-rays and establishing baseline conditions. I didn't know what the tests measured, and the equipment was unlike any diagnostic machines I'd been hooked up to before.

**–Electromyography (EMG) and Thermal Scans:** Network treatments include non-invasive imaging procedures that determine if the spine is misaligned. Nerves generate tiny electrical pulses that travel up and down the central nervous system, carrying messages from the brain to all the body's organs. Disrupted spinal systems result in decreases or increases in electrical impulses. Any changes were measured by temperature fluctuations, providing a better understanding of which areas of my spine needed the most attention.

My tests generated a Core Score based on five factors.

**-Heart Rate Variability:** Heart rates fluctuate throughout the day in response to natural stimuli. Some People also experience various stress levels and higher or lower heart rates. Network techniques have kept me on an even keel.

**-Muscle Tone and Balance:** Tired muscles are less likely to function correctly. The EMG measures muscle condition and determines the energy needed for optimal activity.

**-Range of Motion:** The tests provided insight into the movement of my spine and whether I favored one side over the other or bent over incorrectly. It turned out that the treatments kept my legs the same length by straightening my lower spine.

**-Organ and Gland Control:** The nerves send instructions to my bodily systems. Another test measures changes in spinal temperature and whether any abnormality disrupted the transmitted messages.

**Aggravated and Inflamed Areas:** The Network imaging systems map stress and pain that target the areas for treatment.

After completing my testing, a technician entered my data into the Insight Millennium Subluxation Station. I could see my misalignment and a visual of my spinal health. Clinicians conducted tests periodically. I enhanced my network treatments by adding personal lifestyle changes that support my Noom approach to healthy eating.

**-X-rays:** I was surprised that my posture wasn't as good as it could be. My lower spine was still out of kilter, and my neck views indicated I was a sloucher.

Not only did my back pain subside, but I also credited my overall good health to Network's gentle treatments and my new positive mental attitude. After a year of intensive treatments, I switched to a twice-a-month maintenance plan.

Now that I taped my mouth shut, it meant more oxygen to my brain, and my mind and body were in better balance. I slept more soundly, and my back pain had disappeared.

# Chapter 8

# COVID-19: History Repeats

My life was on cruise control. I had skipped one dental cleaning because my teeth were straighter and I could chew food better. Network was the key to keeping my body in balance. Getting younger was easy. Wouldn't you know it, a global pandemic caused by the Coronavirus (COVID-19) had spread across the Earth. The pandemic resulted in national and international mandates requiring people to self-isolate. That was a big setback because I felt uneasy about going to the dentist or for my Network treatments.

When discussing how diseases spread, three terms frequently come up: epidemic, pandemic, and endemic. The World Health Organization provides the global framework for classifying and monitoring diseases. An epidemic occurs when a disease suddenly increases in a community or region beyond expected levels, such as a flu outbreak in a city or state. A pandemic occurs when an epidemic spreads across multiple countries or continents, affecting a significant portion of the world, as seen with COVID-19. An endemic describes a disease that is regularly present in a specific geographic area or population, such as malaria in parts of sub-Saharan Africa.

Viruses similar to COVID-19 were generally known, but not this strain.

The COVID-19 pandemic reminded me of a smallpox epidemic in the 1920s. I was wary of COVID-19 but not freaked out. Having Medicare coverage offered some peace of mind.

The State of Colorado hadn't yet rescinded the online driver license renewal, which was a positive unintended consequence of the pandemic. The CDC still recommends that people, especially those who are immunocompromised or elderly, get the COVID-19 vaccination boosters. I scheduled an appointment at a Walgreens in Longmont for November 4th. The government also announced that another vaccine, specifically designed for the latest COVID-19 variant, known as Omicron, had been released. I received that version at the same Longmont Walgreens in March 2022.

During the pandemic, people revealed their true selves. It was a panic. As I ventured into 2021, I received my first dose of the Moderna vaccine on February 21, 2021.

Fortunately for me, I'm computer-savvy and was able to get an appointment at the Salud Health Center in Longmont, 20 miles from Boulder. CDC researchers recommended the second and third.

*******

The 2020 election was a heated one. Joe Biden defeated incumbent President Trump, which led to challenges during the ensuing transition, including the federal response to the COVID-19 pandemic. That bottleneck didn't help. The citizenry panicked. The virus spread so quickly that the hit-and-miss efforts to control the disease couldn't keep up.

The conspiracy theory noise championed by Trump continued. The origin of COVID-19 in China was politicized and caused collateral emotional and physical attacks on Asians.

On top of it all, a hodgepodge of political banter received more attention than public health concerns. Trump supporters positioned masking mandates as civil rights violations.

Anti-vaxxers spread rumors claiming vaccine inoculations were secret plots to implant tracking microchips into unsuspecting people. Others believed that hydroxychloroquine (Plaquenil), typically prescribed for arthritis, was the most effective treatment for COVID-19. Trump also speculated that doctors could inoculate patients with Clorox to kill the virus on contact.

Despite the anti-vaccination rhetoric, the Trump administration effectively led the first wave of vaccinations in a military-led effort called "Operation Warp Speed." Food and Drug Administration (FDA) vaccine approvals for Pfizer, Moderna, and Johnson & Johnson occurred in record time.

Regardless, those who contracted the disease were stuck due to a lack of hospital beds. For the rest of us, the ability of states to distribute the vaccine hadn't kept pace with how quickly the FDA approved them. By the end of 2020, fewer than 3 million people had received the vaccine, far short of the federal government's goal to vaccinate 20 million Americans.

*******

Growing younger and digressing two years, I was miserable from a nagging illness. I made an appointment with my doctor for March 10, 2020. She reported, "No improvement really from a month ago. Stop by for a chest X-ray on the way out of the clinic today. Take Prednisone tabs as prescribed for 11 days, then stop. Resume the Flonase and continue the steroid inhaler for now - you can stop both of these in a week or two after your cough has resolved."

Was I an undiagnosed COVID-19 case? Doctors prescribed Prednisone for early COVID-19 patients. In retrospect, I was surprised my doctor didn't order me to get a blood test. I volunteered for the Boulder International Film Festival (BIFF), which was scheduled from March 5th to 8th. My role was to edit videos, documenting the weekend events.

At one of the BIFF opening parties, smartphones went off simultaneously. Was there a child being abducted? No, the University of Colorado reported a COVID-19 case. At the time, information about COVID-19 was limited. Nobody was alarmed. Few people understood why CU sent out a mass notification, and everyone went back to their reveling.

The BIFF was the last major event in Boulder before social isolation mandates. The festival staff had gathered enough basic information to buy nearly all the hand sanitizer in town.

Before the festival on March 2, 2020, I wasn't any better and had a phone consultation with a KP nurse. She reported that I had "Swollen glands, sore throat, no fever, discolored phlegm, was told he should feel better after 3 weeks, but does not."

The month before, I went to see my doctor on February 12th, who reported, "Patient states continued cough since office visit yesterday. Has done sinus rinses and occasionally gets out green mucus plugs. Tender gland on the right side of the neck. Patient remains afebrile (without fever) and states cough is the main concern, and otherwise has been feeling fine." Thinking it was pneumonia, my doctor prescribed antibiotics, Flonase, and a steroid inhaler.

The day before, I had made a doctor's appointment at the KP clinic for February 11th. The doctor said I had bronchitis and instructed me to take cough medicine, acetaminophen, and ibuprofen. Her post-visit notes said, "lung congestion, coughing, and now congestion in his head. Coughs so hard that he can't breathe sometimes, coughing up clearish sputum, but no shortness of breath, only chest pain occurs when coughing too much. He mostly experiences post-nasal drip and frequently blows his nose. Fatigued and achy bones."

*******

In the fall of 2019, I continued with my business as usual and wondered why I was so sick. The initial anecdotal reports and stories reminded me of a movie called *Outbreak* (1995), starring Dustin Hoffman and Rene Russo. In the film, internationally renowned epidemiologists were unable to identify an unknown virus before the rapidly spreading disease was out of control. An illegally imported monkey that escaped from a pet store was the story's inciting incident.

Like in *Outbreak*, the origin of the COVID-19 virus was a mystery. How the disease spread was anyone's guess, with lots of conjecture. The public health community had limited knowledge about symptoms and treatments.

In November, my production partner, Michael, and I caught annoying coughs. We were BIFF volunteers. Michael taught a filmmaking class at the local community college, and we were assembling student crews to document the festival. The small BIFF office, with about a dozen workers screening movies and volunteers sorting boxes, was a potential hot spot for communicable diseases. My cough was so bad that my colleagues banned me from festival meetings.

Interviewing sick people might have caused my illness. On October 10, 2019, when I was contacted by a local nonprofit group, Right Relationship Boulder, inquiring about BCM's ability to document an Indigenous Peoples' Day event that celebrated tribal efforts to return to their traditional homeland and mourned the loss of tribal culture caused by westward expansion.

I loaded up and headed to the Boulder High School venue on the day of the event, where I met up with Michael.

The assignment involved interviews with Arapaho tribal members from the Wind River Reservation in west-central Wyoming and Concho, Oklahoma. The people I interviewed were experiencing symptoms like sneezing, hacking, and coughing. Two of the interviewees were so sick they had to cancel, but I managed to find replacements at the last minute. I got the content I needed.

*******

The COVID-19 pandemic was a case of history repeating itself. A century ago, a smallpox epidemic struck the United States. The deadly virus appeared in over 30 states during the early to mid-1920s. In 1922, there were 28,338 cases and 485 deaths. Those numbers increased to 49,587 and 871 by 1924.

I read a story about the smallpox outbreak in the Twin Cities of Minnesota between October 1924 and May 1925, which resulted in 338 smallpox cases and 25 deaths in St. Paul, as well as 1,160 cases and 350 deaths in Minneapolis.

During the 1920s, science demonstrated the value of vaccination. The anti-vaccination advocates lobbied the U.S. Congress to prevent the Public Health Service from assisting state health authorities in conducting mandatory vaccination programs.

Smallpox has a long history of resistance to vaccination. British people had access to the first smallpox vaccine developed by Edward Jenner in 1796. Cowpox scabs were the initial source for the vaccine. Skeptics feared blindness, deafness, ulcers, and horrific skin lesions known as "cowpox mange." On the far extreme was a fear that vaccinated people would grow hoofs and horns.

Despite the effectiveness of the smallpox vaccine, conspiracy theorists created an anti-vaccination movement that would continue to grow.

In Minnesota, the Anti-Vaccination League was formed by freedom of choice advocates after a smallpox outbreak in 1899–1900 resulted in over 1,000 cases, including 28 deaths in

48 counties. An 1883 Minnesota law required smallpox vaccinations of all school-age children.

In 1903, the anti-vaccination movement convinced the legislature to repeal the law, making compulsory childhood vaccination illegal. Although smallpox vaccinations were almost 100 percent effective, public health officers had no authority to compel people to protect themselves. They could recommend but not mandate the vaccine.

The Twin Cities launched free vaccination clinics starting in November 1924. As the number of deaths increased, one of the local newspapers reported that 17,000 freaked-out people were vaccinated in one day. A week before Christmas 1924, public health officials reported that over half a million residents of Minneapolis and St. Paul had been immunized.

The paper also ran a story in April 1903 about the death of Charles Stevens, secretary of the Minneapolis Anti-Vaccination League. Smallpox was reported as the cause of his death. He and his group falsely purported that smallpox wasn't contagious. A month later, his survivors couldn't collect a $1,000 insurance policy death benefit because, rather than get vaccinated, Stevens waived the smallpox clause in the policy.

Sound familiar? That's because history does repeat itself. Public health and the common good prevailed in the Minnesota smallpox example, and they have continued to do so with COVID-19. The Colorado public health infrastructure finally got on track, although it wasn't like you could walk into your doctor's office and get a shot.

My KP clinic was overwhelmed, and although it stocked the vaccine, it hadn't developed a way to administer it to patients' arms. Drugstore chains and smaller clinics were on the front lines, but getting an appointment was a different story. I searched, found a clinic, and scheduled online.

Staying inside was an inconvenience. I think people who spent most of their time at a job or out socializing had a rude awakening. It turned out that I realized during self-isolation that I didn't go out much, COVID or no COVID. That nation-wide mandate halted my documentary film projects and pro-vided a good excuse to sit in front of my computer and start writing books. Other people who had jobs, spent time with coworkers, or went out on the town learned how dependent they had become on human interactions.

Now that I'm younger, it was time to get on with my life as I continued moving backward to 2018 when I qualified for Medicare.

# Chapter 9

# Cataract Surgery: A Gas, Gas, Gas

Just before the COVID-19 pandemic spread worldwide, the Greatest Rock and Roll Band in the World, the Rolling Stones, was playing at the Denver Broncos football stadium on August 13, 2019. Mick Jagger had a heart attack months earlier and had to reschedule the "No Filters Tour."

"This was probably the last time I would have a chance to see the Stones, and I'm half blind," I thought. I went online and found that a few tickets in the nosebleed section were still available. After stewing about it, I bought two high-priced nosebleed seats.

I invited my now estranged friend, who advised me about periodontal surgery. I was surprised I could see enough to drive. I stopped by to pick her up. Before we took off, she knew of my eye surgery and handed me a marijuana vape wand. Being the cautious type, she drove.

Back in the olden days, when pot use and possession were felonies, there was an urban legend that when asked about smoking weed, the medical explanation was that it cured glaucoma. I'll be darned if it didn't clear up my eyesight for the next two hours Mick was on stage. The set began with *Street Fightin' Man* and ended 19 tunes later with *Satisfaction*.

I was able to see the show as if it were 1981, the first time I saw the Stones in the Pontiac Silverdome near Detroit. As it turned out, drummer Charlie Watts died soon after the Denver gig while the tour was still happening. I'm glad I took the risk and saw the Stones. The show was a gas, gas, gas.

*******

Before the concert, I used my Medicare benefits for the second time on August 7, 2019.  My poor vision had finally become too problematic, even though needing cataract surgery wasn't related to the trait I inherited from my Mom.

My left eye had always been the weakest of my body parts, with a vision rating of 20/400.  If both my eyes were that bad, I'd be legally blind.  Eyewear has improved over the years. When the contact lens industry ironed the wrinkles out of its products, I began wearing semi-soft ones more than my glasses.  Those helped immensely when I became a filmmaker.

I didn't want my doctor to force me to stop driving like my dad.  That's a decision I want to make myself.  His vision had worsened. Handing over his keys was a reverse rite of passage for him, compared to the freedom he first experienced when earning his driver's license as a kid.  Losing it felt like a sign of disability.  On the other hand, I can't wait for the day I can stop driving.  It's dangerous out here, with all the old folks like me on the road forgetting to signal, running stop signs, and tailgating.

When I went in for my annual eye test in 2018, my KP optometrist told me I was developing cataracts.  Based on my experience with still cameras in Lander, I noticed that the images I saw through my movie camera were fuzzy.

"I think it's time for you to consider cataract surgery," he said while shining a bright light through a prism to examine my eyes.  "Your lens is cloudier than it's been. I'll make a referral to one of our ophthalmologists."

Cataracts are thin coatings that form on the lens of the eye. I wasn't confident that my eyes could consistently keep an image in focus, but it looked fuzzy.  Because of that hesitancy, I used the "automatic" mode on my movie cameras.

Then there was the night vision impairment.  When I drove toward oncoming traffic, there were halos around the headlights, and the same was true for the traffic signals.  It was a blur, but I was still able to make out shapes.

The lens of the eye is situated behind the colored part called the iris. Just like a camera, the lens focuses light that passes through the pupil to create a clear image on the retina, the light-sensitive layer at the back of the eye, similar to a movie screen.

My eye lenses became thicker and less flexible.  Lens proteins and fibers broke down and coated my lenses.  Over time, the layer of deteriorated lens crud became denser.  When light entered my eye, I saw a fuzzy image projected onto the retina as the image passed through my dirty lens.

Like most people, my cataracts developed in both eyes.  The fogginess hadn't become severe enough to warrant removal. I was required to have a consultation with him.  Dr. Letko explained the procedure to me, which would take less than an hour for both eyes, and informed me that I would need a designated driver.

"Both at once? That's unusual." I explained the procedure to my upstairs neighbor, Lindy.  She was a nurse for a cataract surgeon.  "The general practice is to do one at a time. That's so doctors and insurance companies can charge for two surgeries and two co-pays."

My greatest hesitation was choosing between monovision and 20/20. Before the surgery, I wore contacts and glasses corrected to "monovision," meaning my left eye was corrected for close vision, and my right eye, which had 20/40 vision, was corrected for distance. Monovision also meant I wouldn't need reading glasses. I could see pretty well with my new eyes, but the doctor upsold me into a pair of progressive vision glasses that did improve my distance and close-up sight.

"Did you have 'lazy eye'?" Dr. Letko asked about my left eye.

"It looks to me like it might have been a mild case. Your eye compensated for it. That's why your vision is so bad."

"My cousin had a lazy eye," I responded. "Maybe it was genetic."

*******

I have astigmatism, and my new left eye lens supposedly had a hefty co-pay. I showed up on the day of my surgery, braced with my credit card in hand.

"So, what do I owe today?" The clerk flipped through a stack of papers, then shook her head.

"Nothing. You're all set."

"Nothing?" I said, certain there must be a mistake.

"That's what it says."

Humans still handle much of the Medicare paperwork. Later, I realized my doctor or someone in the benefits office must have downcoded my procedure, submitting it as though I was scheduled to receive the standard lens. The system had quietly bent the rules to ease my burden.

Remember to check your paperwork and benefits before surgery, was my lesson learned.

*******

Dr. Letko required that I have a designated driver. That task fell on Diana. She accompanied me to the pre-operation cubicle, where a nurse loaded me onto an eye surgery stretcher.

The nurse administered local anesthetic eye drops before rolling me into the operating room, where another nurse covered my face with a surgical drape. The doctor came by and made a small incision into my left cornea, which covered the iris, then removed the natural lens and replaced it with an artificial one.  I saw him wearing a magnifier, shielding his face with the paper, but the work was tedious.  I sensed his hands gently trembling.  He took off, returned a few minutes later, and did the second eye.

I was in the operating room for no more than 30 minutes. There were patients lined up on gurneys like airplanes awaiting their turn to take off.  Every few minutes, the next patient taxied into the outpatient surgery room.

That was it. A nurse rolled back to the pre-operation area where my ride was waiting.  I could see pretty well when the dilating eye drops wore off.  Since it was a local anesthetic, I was up and about, but my vision was blurry.

*******

Speaking of gas, gas, gas, as an aside, in case you were wondering, the first time I used my Medicare benefits was for my second colonoscopy. That was seven years after my first when I turned 65. That preventative procedure was supposedly "new and improved." The difference was a kit with all the ingredients, ready for me to pick up at the KP pharmacy. The colon cleanser seemed to have more cleansing power. I had quite a bit more leakage.

SSV has a medical closet. Since we're all older, we've accumulated a stash of walkers, wheelchairs, and shower benches. There's a shelf with other supplies, such as adult diapers. After being released from the hospital, patients grab anything consumable, including opened packages of diapers.

I'm glad that I introduced myself to a few of those for the drive to the KP outpatient clinic to protect the car seat. I had a choice between light and heavy anesthesia. I chose light, but that was enough to knock me out for the procedure. Everything must have come out all right, since I woke up bright-eyed and bushy-tailed.

*******

Having cataracts removed was the best healthcare decision I'd made to date, but it's always something. Because of my glaucoma risk, I have my eyes checked often. The latest results indicated that my internal eyeball pressure had increased. The doctor prescribed me eye drops that I use twice a day.

"If I've been at risk for glaucoma for many years, why are you now prescribing me the drops?" I asked.

"When you're young, you don't need them. When you're old, the likelihood of problems is greater. Eye drops don't stop your aging."

Although in my case, it was the un-aging process.

Up until I died and was reborn, I'd religiously dripped the drops in my eyes. My doctor did say that they lose their effectiveness, not because of the medicine, but because of the patient's inability to administer them, as well as forgetfulness. Luckily, the eye drops would be a phase. I wondered if I'd have trouble with my new lenses as I became more youthful.

The eye drops hadn't improved the pressure in my left eyeball, and my glaucoma ophthalmologist, Dr. Quinn, prescribed a third set. When I was in my 80s, I set a reminder on my iPhone. My caregiver didn't have to deal with that little task.

If you're one of those "age is just a number" adherents who think that getting cataract surgery will make you feel older, I have a news flash. Cataract surgery, colonoscopies, and rheumatoid arthritis are badges of honor that no 40-year-old can take from you. As I grew younger, I appreciated my old age experiences, including seeing the Rolling Stones a total of six times.

Chapter 10

# The FORCE: Add Years to Life

Having lived at Silver Sage Village, where my lifestyle was collaborative, I wondered if forming closer interpersonal relationships would translate into better health. My mouth and throat no longer dried out when I mouth-breathed. The Network community complemented my traditional Western healthcare options. Being treated in the presence of other patients added to my wellness. I was able to see the world more clearly with my new eyes, and I missed out on colon cancer.

SSV intentionally facilitates neighborly interactions. Meeting up with friends, gathering with family on holidays, and relaxing at neighborhood or workplace parties are activities for exchanging thoughts, team building, and emotional support.

One of my neighbors circulated a flyer about a study at the University of Colorado that measured the influence of social interaction and physical activity on brain function and life expectancy among older and sedentary adults. I was curious about how my experiences in intentional communities may have affected my health, so I signed up to participate in the Fitness Older Adults and Resting-state Connectivity Enhancement (FORCE) study.

"We're an aging population, and as we grow older, the challenge is making the extra years quality ones," Angela Bryan, University of Colorado professor of Social Psychology and Neuroscience, explained. She was the FORCE study's principal investigator. "As neuroscientists, we wondered how the brain can be a part of those effects. The experiment aimed to determine if physical exercise helped participants maintain their quality of life by improving brain function."

I was an older adult who didn't exercise much and was qualified to participate. I had to give up my yoga practice during the study. First, I underwent a test to establish my baseline stamina on a treadmill. I then had my memory checked by recalling quiz answers. The technician scanned me with a Magnetic Resonance Imaging (MRI) machine. I was on my back and passed through a magnetic field that produced a three-dimensional image of my brain. I think I'll splice the images together with my colonoscopy movie.

I walked on a treadmill for 30 minutes at 2.5 mph three times a week for 16 weeks. Afterward, I was retested and underwent another MRI scan to assess whether my brain function and physical stamina had improved.

"There are plenty of research studies that show that interpersonal relationships powerfully influence our long-term health in positive ways," Professor Bryan noted. "We added physical activity to the experiment."

In 2016, I produced a documentary about my experiences and observations entitled *Aging Gratefully: The Power of Good Health and Good Neighbors*. Throughout the project, I spoke with experts and individuals who live in cohousing about their relationships, physical exercise, and experiences in creating an intentional neighborhood. Some people choose to be isolated because they prefer to be by themselves. For example, a person may have a large circle of friends yet still feel alone.

The relatively new Germantown Commons community opened its doors in Nashville, Tennessee, in 2015. I interviewed several residents there for my documentary.

A neighbor named Doug discovered that collaborating with others was more effective than working in isolation in a private apartment. He said members would often ride their bikes, walk to a baseball game, or share a meal at a nearby restaurant. "I'm much more in touch with people. We talk about problems and solutions. That's been very supportive."

"If she doesn't see me for a few days, Suzanne comes right over to check on me." A resident named Essie had a pulmonary embolism. She shared a dog with her neighbor, Suzanne, who happened by and called 911. "Having other people around to provide support is a big benefit of living here."

"I didn't want to grow older by myself," Ginger said. "I was talking to a friend the other day. She said I had changed. I'm usually a very anxious person, but my life has become less stressful here. We're all very active, which helps. Germantown Commons is near the Cumberland River, where I can drop my kayak."

During the community's construction, Chris served as the liaison between the community and the general contractor. "My wife and I ended up being very active during the early stages. I didn't want to come home and mow the lawn for recreation. I wanted to go for a hike and bike ride."

Their niece, Sarah, and her son, Harry, are community members. "My neighbors are very helpful. When I need to run inside for a minute, a neighbor will watch Harry. A neighbor gave me a gallon of milk that saved me a trip to the store."

*******

Robert Putnam wrote a book about social isolation, *Bowling Alone: The Collapse and Revival of American Community*

(2000). He examines the decline of face-to-face social networks and the resulting decline in civic engagement.

Two decades later, social isolation remains a significant health hazard.

The FORCE study is ongoing, but the preliminary results are promising. "Interacting with people relaxes us. It increases the chance we won't worry about things, not be stressed," Dr. Bryan said. "Social interactions with people and being in clubs have positive effects. In our FORCE study, we are seeing improvement in brain function as a result of physical activity."

A national survey of 309,000 people found that loneliness and social isolation increased the likelihood of death by 50 percent, which is as deadly as smoking 15 cigarettes a day.

I'm not much for rigorous exercise. My Bolder Boulder 10K walk-jog, which includes recording the music and festivities around the race, is the extent of my aerobic activity.

"For a lot of people, being active isn't that rewarding," Dr. Bryan said. "They do it. They know it's healthy, but it's not fun. Doing a physical activity with people, making it a point to do a hike with other people in a social setting, can make it a lot more rewarding than slogging through on your own."

Nurturing positive relationships with others requires no specialized gear or equipment and can happen through everyday life activities, such as taking a walk or attending a book club meeting.

Even if you don't choose an intentional community like SSV, living, get off the couch, meet people in your neighborhood, join a club and volunteer, attend family gatherings, whether you get along with your relatives or not, or do any other spontaneous group activities.

I had forgotten about the importance of community until I remembered what I had learned from participating in the FORCE study and from the Germantown cohousers.

# Chapter 11

# Little Yoga Studio: Down Dog

By Labor Day 2014, I was still very weak and wasn't sure how to get into better shape. I didn't want to join a private gym or the North Boulder Recreation Center because of the price. For what I needed, both were overkill.

I was picking something up at McGuckin Hardware in early September 2014, the Sunday afternoon before Labor Day, when I noticed the Little Yoga Studio next door. I was still in pretty bad shape. My PHN encircled the right side of my head and face. Despite my physical therapy, I was still very weak, and my joints didn't flex very well.

"That's what I need. Yoga would be perfect," I thought. I wanted to maintain endurance and flexibility, not develop muscle bulk. I didn't want to be like some athletes who worked hard to maintain their peak physical condition only to lose it all when they stopped working out and lapsed into flabbiness as they aged.

There was a woman inside working on the computer at the front desk. The studio was closed, but she told me to take a schedule from the plastic box by the door. The prices were very reasonable because the studio was "little." There were no locker rooms or showers, only two rudimentary changing areas and cubbies for personal items. I liked that it was a very trust-ing atmosphere.

When I first moved to Boulder, I watched an early morning yoga program on cable TV. I did that for a while and gained some experience with the basic poses. When the instructor in-troduced weights and other equipment, I stopped practicing. The breadth of my knowledge knew the difference between up-ward-facing and downward-facing dogs.

Since my body was out of whack, I thought yoga would be more balanced than going to a gym, plus I only needed a mat. I had sticker shock when I saw that mats cost as much as $85.

There was one for $10 at one of the local discount stores. You would think a mat is a mat, but in fact, they are different, and quality matters. I get obsessed with my activities and have since upgraded my mat to a name brand.

I have two mats. One folds flat and is easily tossed into a suitcase when traveling. The other is thicker, denser, and better for my knobby knees and bony butt.

I wanted to get stronger, more flexible, and more focused on the present. The week after Labor Day, I took my first class. I didn't know what to expect, as it was my first time participat-ing in organized yoga practice.

The instructors I selected were the more meditative ones. I have learned that the Americanized versions of yoga are more secular and distinct from their traditional roots, which span 5,000 years in South Asia.

A friend of mine, Ravi, publishes a magazine that covers es-oteric topics like yoga. He wrote an article about India reclaim-ing its yoga. Western-based yoga moved away from the original spiritual intentions.

Ravi and I met to discuss my story idea about the American $9 billion yoga industry, which includes studios with dressing rooms and showers, as well as clothing, mats, water bottles, equipment, and food - anything that a yoga business could brand.

"I don't like how yoga has been over-commercialized," Ravi said. "Any yoga is better than no yoga."

That put the kibosh on my original story idea. I ended up writing a couple of scripts for the Little Yoga Studio and produced informational videos for them.

My initial reasons for attending yoga class several times a week were health and medical-related. I didn't anticipate integrating the spiritual aspect of yoga into my life. I wanted to pick up where my physical therapist (PT) left off by improving my stamina and flexibility without gaining excessive muscle mass. Yoga has had a profoundly positive impact on my life.

I practiced for two or three days, then took a day of recovery time in between. It was part of my weekly routine, and when I can connect physical body motion to my brain.

COVID-19 closed the studio, and the classes moved online. That was good since I didn't have to spend 30 minutes driving back and forth from home. Being part of my yoga community was beneficial, both in a virtual and face-to-face setting.

*******

One Little Yoga Studio instructor gave short *dharma* lessons at the beginning of the class, setting intentions for approaching life based on physical and metaphysical variables.

The teacher mused that stressful times, such as holidays, push everyone to be extroverted, which can be stressful when dealing with friends and family. For introverts like me, it was fitting that the day's yoga practice focused on attitudinal grounding. It was beneficial for my mental and physical well-being.

The last pose is lying on your back and relaxing while remaining conscious, known as *savasana*, or the corpse pose. After an hour of fighting with Warrior 2, folding forward, and balancing on one foot like a tree, I welcomed the quiet time.

I'm lousy at meditation, but lying on my back is an excellent time to think about stuff and eventually clear my head. I've been keenly aware of the world around me and entered self-imposed hospice: silence amid the noise.

I became introspective, lived my life to the fullest, and kept telling my truths, story by story, sentence by sentence, and word by word, to paraphrase Anne Lamott and her memoir *Bird by Bird* (1994) about her life as a writer.

One day, my *savasana* was notably silent. My mind was clear, and I waited for the teacher to release us with a gentle namaste. Before I knew it, my eyes opened, and I noticed the yoga studio Zoom room was closed after my half-hour nap. I hope the teacher didn't call 911 and report me lying motionless on my mat in front of the webcam.

When I began my yoga practice, I wasn't sure if it would improve or worsen my health. I became more flexible, but my lung capacity was still low. I had a conversation with my pulmonologist, Dr. Kinnard, about the possibility of a lung transplant if things didn't improve.

Prednisone was the only solution Western medicine had to offer. That made me uneasy, not to mention the chronic pain that persisted after the shingle blisters healed. I was one of the few who developed PHN. In my case, the left side of my scalp and face was numb and painful. Yoga couldn't do anything about that.

Now what?

Chapter 12

# Traditional Chinese Medicine: Healthy Needling

Yoga was a good choice to supplement Western medicine with a meditative component. I explored another alternative practice because, in May 2014, I realized that KP doctors were pretty good at handling obvious health issues, like stitching wounds, splinting broken bones, and prescribing remedial drugs for measurable conditions like high blood pressure. Looking back, my doctors were all a little vague with me and wouldn't give specific answers.

That was frustrating, and I decided to try Traditional Chinese Medicine (TCM), a practice that has been evolving for thousands of years. Practitioners employ a range of psychological and physical treatments, including multiple forms of acupuncture, herbal remedies, and martial arts.

Martial art forms like *tai chi* and *qi gong* incorporate slow, meditative postures and breathing techniques, which enhance mental focus. For older people, internal martial arts practices can help balance and reduce knee and back pain.

I was frustrated by my Western healthcare team's hit-and-miss approach. My doctors made diagnoses based on educated guesses, at best, for medical conditions they couldn't see with the naked eye.

"Try this dosage for a while and check back," my doc advised. "That didn't work? Let's take an X-ray and see if there's a problem in there."

Despite the vague diagnoses, the KP managed care network is a known quantity. I can pick any KP service provider. I've heard about the runaround some patients get in "siloed" managed care services, hoping their PCP remembered to make a referral, searching for in-network specialists, and driving from place to place for appointments.

I have a designated PCP, but I also have access to all the doctors, nurse practitioners, and physician assistants in his group and have gotten to know them all. If I had an immediate need, there are time slots where someone could schedule me on the spur of the moment.

Dr. Kinnard had me breathe supplemental oxygen for another four months. Every summer after that, I made an appointment to get checked out. It's not that there were any new issues with my breathing. We had a strong bond, and it was nice to catch up. He and his wife were supporters of the BIFF. We would run into each other outside of his work life at the film festival opening night reception.

We recalled the time when Manor Care had released me from rehab. I was still pretty sick, and we discussed options, including a lung transplant. I asked why he didn't recommend pulling the plug on me.

"I had a feeling you were going to make it," Kinnard said. "You ended up having such a miraculous recovery. I don't know what I would have discussed at medical conferences."

Dr. Lookner, my PCP, was amazed at my recovery. He had no vision for my future, nor did he venture a guess about whether my lungs would deteriorate after I quit the steroids or if I would be on supplemental oxygen for the rest of my life. As long as my regular doctors were pretty knowledgeable about medical game theory, I decided to incorporate alternative medical practices.

*******

My Western rehabilitation was effective, helping me return to my everyday life. The residual shingles pain that settled on my left scalp was bothersome. The fabric swatch that patched my ulcer constricted my abdomen, and I couldn't eat as much as before. I used to take "all you can eat" as a challenge. Yoga helped keep my muscles loose. My next experiment was to integrate TCM.

When I came to Boulder in 1993, a Chinese acupuncture doctor named Dr. Pao treated me. I had developed gout from kicking too many soccer balls. I thought it was a bit over the top when he bled my right big toe with lancets the size of ice picks. My toe joint loosened up after he let the blood out. I still have a mild case that I treat with Allopurinol.

TCM gained widespread recognition in the United States in 1971. That was when *New York Times* reporter James Reston traveled to China to cover Secretary of State Kissinger's advance trip that paved the Way for an upcoming visit by President Nixon.

Reston came down with acute appendicitis. Local surgeons used acupuncture as anesthesia during the appendectomy and after the surgery to control post-operative pain.

Based on the vague comments from my doctors, it was clear that Western medicine had run its course. Scar tissue and fluids still restricted my breathing, and the PHN wasn't going away anytime soon. Dr. Pao was still in business, and I made an appointment. He prescribed a goopy plaster infused with herbs that he squished over the healing blisters.

At that time, his office was in a strip mall. Behind the counter were giant jars of herbs, dried animal parts, and insects. He kept track of patients by their first names. Behind the check-in counter, he had cordoned off the treatment rooms with bed sheets pinned overhead on clothesline cords.

Every treatment included a tea blend of ground-up herbs and critters for whatever was ailing me. The foul-smelling powder smelled like rotting fowl. I added it to my coffee because it nullified the flavor of the herbs and improved my morning Joe.

I didn't think his treatment was effective this time to improve my PHN or my breathing.

Someone told me about the Southwest Acupuncture College (SWAC). Students provided a variety of treatment modalities under the supervision of college faculty members. In May 2014, I switched to the SWAC, which was like the KP HMO. I could pick from several practitioners under the same roof.

Choosing an acupuncturist was like when I decided on a PCP. I got to know the supervising doctor and their student practitioners. I had strong connections with some. There's quite a bit of energy transfer between my physical condition and how the practitioner places the needles. Students come and go, but I've had good luck with three students in particular. I want to be one of their first patients when they pass their certification exams.

I tried quite a few of the treatments for my PHN and my clogged-up lungs. The most effective for me was *tuina* (pronounced twee-nah), a combination of needle therapy and physical hand manipulation. Another was *guasha* (pronounced gwah-shah). Practitioners rub the smooth edge of a ceramic spoon or stone over various locations on the back, helping to raise stagnant blood to the surface.

Blood stagnation is a TCM term referring to the slowing or blocking of blood flow and circulation in various parts of the body, which is considered a contributing factor to pain. It is generally localized and can result from overuse or injury, such as sprains or bruising.

*Guasha* is similar to cupping, made famous by Olympic swimmer Michael Phelps, who had a medical practitioner place cups on the skin and vacuum out the air, leaving distinct red bruises. TCM also practices cupping, but the vacuum is created by placing a flaming piece of cotton under the glass cup, which creates a vacuum that allows the rim to adhere to the skin.

"This college has much to offer to the wider community," I wondered while in the middle of treatment with the clinic manager named Joanne. We were acquainted from one of our mutual past lives, advocating for the citywide vote to end indoor smoking. While she walked me to the front, I mentioned that the SWAC had a pretty good story.

"I agree," she said. We sat down in the lobby. "I'll mention this to a few others. Come up with some ideas and a budget. Videos would be a powerful way to give prospective students and the public a means to kick the acupuncture tires. " In exchange for several informational video programs about the various treatments offered by the SWAC clinic, I received acupuncture treatments.

*******

The X-ray Dr. Kinnard ordered in March 2014 showed scar tissue and fluids that still restricted my breathing. Over the next few months, I had various TCM treatments before another X-ray. When I compared the two images, a remarkable improvement was evident. I don't know if the treatments were effective, but telling people that acupuncture was a miracle was more fun.

According to acupuncture theory, the lungs and skin are closely related, as they are both exposed to air. "Whatever it is that they're doing for you over there, keep doing it," Dr. Kinnard said during my first check-up after he looked at the chest X-ray he took after 12 weeks of acupuncture treatment.

My lung condition improved, and he tapered me off the steroids. I immersed myself in Eastern medicine after my first visit to SWAC and learned a great deal about alternative therapies.

Becoming a part of the TCM community has since been a good diversion. The intangible benefits of documentary filmmaking include getting behind the scenes and meeting new people.

I gained some new insights, particularly from the students. For many, they were reinventing themselves and beginning new careers. I could relate to that, mainly because I ended up trading script writing and video production services for acupuncture treatments.

One of the SWAC student practitioners was also an instructor at the Little Yoga Studio. Her goal was to set up a yoga practice that also offered acupuncture. That sounded like a good combination. Alternative health practices would be a welcome change from the hit-and-miss Western medical treatments and advice I'd received before.

# Chapter 13

# PTSD: Setbacks Are Relative

The FORCE study reinforced my belief that being around people serves as a buffer against loneliness. Joining the Little Yoga Studio and adopting TCM complemented my goal to live a longer, healthier, and more physically fit life.

Running in the Bolder Boulder 10K every Memorial Day, along with 50,000 of my closest friends, had always been a benchmark of my stamina.

The annual race is as much a pageant as a running event, featuring a citizens' race that attracts over 50,000 wheelchair racers, runners, and walkers. My acid test in 2014 was whether I could complete my usual task of documenting the music along the route and completing the citizen's race.

The challenge was occupational therapy. I hauled a camera and tripod around and took footage of all the bands and entertainment along the route that snaked through the middle of town and ended in Folsom Field, where the University of Colorado Buffaloes football team plays its games.

It was always exhilarating to enter the stadium and be cheered on by thousands of adoring fans who had finished ahead of me. The citizen's race is a lot of fun. Bands play on the front lawns of houses along the route. Some residents

**77**

along the route set up make-shift Slip 'n Slides. Others handed out cups of the other energy drink: beer, and samples of the other power bar: bacon, to the less serious runners.

By the time I slowed down to take a selfie with Elvis at the 7-Eleven parking lot, shake a leg with the belly dancers, take a few seconds recording each of the musical acts, grab a few Doritos and wash them down with a sip of beer, I was still able to finish the race before the mop-up crew cut off the stragglers from finishing.

All went well, but I needed to take a few deep tokes of oxygen going up the steep Folsom Street hill into the stadium. I carried my purse, which contained a small green oxygen bottle and the regulator. My oxygen saturation was around 80 percent, which was pretty good, considering it had been in the 60s and 70s when I returned from rehab.

In retrospect, running-walking the Bolder Boulder probably wasn't the wisest thing to do. Hauling the camera didn't help my balance. I could have taken a tumble along the way.

Even when healthy, I didn't do much training for the race. Before 2014, pounding my feet on the pavement strained my hip, leg, and ankle joints, but nothing a little Advil wouldn't fix. After the race, I noticed that my lighter weight was immediately apparent, as my inner knees didn't ache, but compared to the months before, it felt like progress.

Maybe I was fooling myself. Sit-ups were still painful because of scarring from the leaky intestinal ulcer patched with a piece of fabric sewn into me and stuck onto my abdominal wall. My legs may not have ached, but they were still weak, and I still gasped for breath after simple tasks like taking out the trash.

********

Finishing the Bolder Boulder wasn't an isolated feat. I had spent the spring testing myself in small ways.  As part of an occupational therapy project, I assembled a crew and produced a short movie for the Wyoming Film Office contest.

The production included writing the script, casting two characters, finding a location, and assembling a crew. The venue was a performance stage for plays in Arvada, a Denver suburb east of Boulder, owned by one of the cast members. The Director of Photography was the guy who led my substitute Boulder International Film Festival crew. He was better on a stationary set.

My project took place after a major snowstorm had passed. I needed to transport myself and the gear in my VW Eurovan. I recruited a volunteer Production Assistant to help schlep the equipment. I started driving again because the movie location was in Arvada. It was the first time I had started the Eurovan in three months. The door was frozen shut, but once I climbed up into the driver's seat, the ignition turned over right away.

Driving probably wasn't that great of an idea, especially if I suddenly had to stop and slam on the brakes. By this time, I had also been issued a blue and white disabled driver parking tag, which hung from the rearview mirror. It was an adventure to see what it was like to park in the handicapped spots legally.

Suddenly, everyone wanted me to drive to various places since I could get close-in parking. I gained an appreciation for people who had the permanent handicap tags, and made a point to confront drivers idling in a marked spot where they would be parked for "only a minute."

The shoot reminded me of who I was before hospitals took over my life. I still felt helpless. Not being able to work due to my health was frustrating. I was in a financial bind.

*******

I'd been a longtime member of the BIFF board of directors. Ron, the event producer, and I typically produced tribute videos for the BIFF celebrity guests. Festival organizers hadn't yet named anyone, but at the last minute, actor Shirley MacLaine accepted the invitation to attend.

The week before the festival weekend, Ron and I collaborated on a reel with Shirley's career highlights. I received a stipend for that work, which was helpful. It was the first money I'd made in three months.

Even though I was still wheelchair-bound, my first public event was on March 5th for the opening night of BIFF 2014. My other responsibility was to provide a production crew to document the talk-backs at the Boulder Theater.

I wanted to check in and see how the replacements were performing. My friend and film production colleague, Michael, had recommended a producer with good credentials, but he turned out to be all camera and no news experience and failed to fulfill as promised. That was a bummer.

I dragged myself to the BIFF to watch the MacLaine tribute. My caregiver, Diana, loaded me up in a wheelchair in front of the Hotel Boulderado, where BIFF held the opening night reception. Riding as a wheelchair user was an eye-opener. While most people could walk straight to the elevator, Diana wheeled me around a circuitous route to get there.

The little bumps and steep humps were not noticeable when trodden upon, but, in some cases, were impossible to navigate in a wheelchair. After some reveling, we wheeled two blocks to the Boulder Theater. I stashed the wheelchair and successfully walked into the main theater. Several friends and well-wishers greeted me before I tipped over backward.

My friend Don caught me.

That was enough fun for one night. I stayed through the MacLaine video and interview when the lights went down. She nixed any video recording of her talk, and the inadequate in-house three-camera crew was off the hook. That was a relief. I was also relieved that I didn't have to respond to comments like, "I was meaning to come visit you ..." or "I feel so sorry you had to go through all that ..." My friends and colleagues were more mindful than I would have imagined.

*******

Before BIFF, my outings were small. I moped around the house before Super Bowl XLVIII was played on February 2, 2014, shortly after I had returned to Silver Sage Village. I tested my strength by wheeling myself out of the condo and to the Common House for the first time. I hadn't noticed all the bumps and small obstacles on the sidewalk until I rolled over them on my way to watch the big game on the big screen TV.

I poked my head into the Media Room. The best part was nobody doted over my return. If you have friends or family in the hospital or recovering at home, check in with them and ask how they would like to be treated. As for me, talk to me like you always have and spare me the crossword puzzle magazines.

Someone did fetch me a plate of nachos and other Super Bowl fare. I stayed for the first half but bid my neighbors farewell because the hose I had sticking out of my abdomen started to leak. It wasn't that great a game. The Seahawks trounced the Broncos 43–8.

I understood the reason why I ended up living in the co-housing community. What surprised me most was that, all of a sudden, my neighbors brought over covered dishes and stopped by to say hello. That was when I realized that the heart of cohousing was intentional caring and sharing.

I appreciated their gestures, but I could only eat so many tuna casseroles. I suggested that nonperishable items would be better. One of the neighbors collected money to defray Diana's commuting costs while driving to the hospital in Lafayette and the rehab center in Denver.

*******

It was good to be back home. My reentry had started when the Manor Care Rehabilitation Center in Denver had released me when I was able to wheel myself into the bathroom and wipe my butt.

Michael picked me up after two weeks at the Manor Care Rehabilitation Center in Denver and drove me to Silver Sage Village. He wheeled me into the Common House. It was good to be on parole and out of the confines of the healthcare prison system.

My insurance benefit provided for a few hours of in-home therapy.  A physical therapist came by the condo and assigned me to curl hand weights. When I started, I could barely lift 1 pound.  She taught me how to walk again and get up if I fell, and I did, when I became overconfident and my knees collapsed from under me while walking up a step on the sidewalk behind my house.

After my ordeal, I noticed people walking with a hitch in their get-along and wondered if I should say something like, "Looks like you should see a chiropractor or physical therapist.  " That was when I set a goal to continue my routine and obtain a press pass for the Bolder Boulder 10K.

An occupational therapist retrained me to perform day-to-day tasks. She showed me how to pack the refrigerator and place things in the cupboard to minimize my range of motion.  She showed me how to put the milk jug in the fridge to reduce the range of motion and waltz around the lines on the kitchen floor to help me regain my sense of balance.

Because old folks populated SSV, there was a store of rehabilitation equipment, such as a shower seat and one of those plastic gizmos that raised the toilet level. Those came in handy. My bed was a low-slung futon that I still use to this day.

Dr. Kinnard ordered the oxygen delivery service to drop off a noisy machine that concentrated oxygen and delivered it directly through a plastic tube into my nose, allowing me to free myself from dragging around the heavy green cylinders. I was also fitted with a black "purse" for a small oxygen tank that I could sling over my shoulder.

Being wheelchair bound and having to breathe supplemental oxygen were rights of passage. I became more aware of others in similar situations and became conversational about tricked-out electric wheelchairs and small, lightweight oxygen concentrators.

Dr. Lookner had me eating and drinking carbohydrates. Even though I was at risk for diabetes, gaining back the lost weight was more important. I still had trouble digesting solid food. Quarts of Ensure protein drinks became my staple. I mixed them with fruit and vegetables to make smoothies. By May, I was still weak.

My occupational and physical therapists couldn't do anything more. Besides, the insurance benefit expired. When I re-learned how to walk and could lift five pounds, my benefits had run out, and KP turned me loose.

*******

I hadn't been home a week before the bills started piling up. I owed around $16,000 for my deductibles and a few thousand for out-of-network expenses. Those were a big shock, but compared to the $98,000 total cost of a month in the hospital, two surgeries, and then two weeks at the rehab center, that was a pretty good deal, but it should have been less.

My time at Manor Care in Denver was fully covered, which was good.

Needless to say, my year-long health crisis greatly affected my life. I became more impatient with people and what I now considered their petty quirks, and I linked my indifference to Post Traumatic Stress Disorder (PTSD) caused by my medical bills and ongoing pain.

One structural issue with health insurance was the rise of high-deductible plans. They look good on paper because they keep monthly premiums low, but they shift enormous risk onto patients if something goes wrong.

My own story is proof. I became deathly ill in December 2013 with an $8,000 deductible plan. I exhausted that amount within the first couple of days. Since I wasn't discharged from the hospital and rehab until January 31, 2014, the new year brought a fresh $8,000 deductible.

Same illness. Same stay.

Two deductibles before insurance started helping is a design flaw, not just bad luck. I've heard that 60 percent of personal bankruptcies are linked to medical bills. I was part of the 20 percent of people impacted by the cost of health-scare.

There wasn't much time for insurance coverage counseling. Plus, I was on drugs, and my healthcare advocacy support system had other things to do besides handle my health insurance re-enrollment paperwork. My doctors didn't consider costs, as their goal was to help me stay within the system's parameters.

Sometimes, that meant going outside my KP network for goods and services. Thinking about that wasn't on their radar. I was sick, and my life was changing rapidly and unpredictably. I couldn't afford to let things slip through the cracks. Next time, I'll try to pay closer attention. By the time I came up for air, I was $16,000+ in the hole.

*******

By late summer 2014, life was edging back toward normal, though "normal" now meant rolling suitcases up stairs with an oxygen tank in tow. I noticed that many public places aren't universally accessible after I arose from my wheelchair.

While I was still recuperating but working, I stayed at a historic bed and breakfast in Cheyenne. To get past the wrought iron gate, there were two concrete steps to climb up to the yard, then four concrete steps to get to the front porch.

Once inside, I had to navigate my rolling suitcase, an oxygen tank, and six stairs to the first landing, then four more stairs to the second landing.

Working on my own has the advantage of having no direct boss. The downside was that unless I hired them, I had no colleagues around to lift my oxygen tank out of the back seat. Friends will help out to a certain extent, as with personal favors like checking the mail and feeding the cat.

However, when asked to perform tasks related to their job, that's a different kind of assistance. While returning to my new routine, Michael and my estranged friend, and Rolling Stones fan, helped tie up my loose ends.

I wasn't making any money, and the medical bills piled up. I kept the vendors off my back by paying them a little at a time, but the debt collection letters soon began to arrive in my mailbox.

"Rather than pay me, pay off your bills," a bankruptcy attorney advised. "I can't do much for you. Your debt is small compared to most of my clients."

All the bills had maxed out my credit card debt limit, so I applied to increase it. Then, I paid off my hospital bill, deductible, and various out-of-network vendors. After being discharged from the hospital, it was a financially challenging time, and I hadn't finished my therapy at Manor Care in Denver.

The healthcare industrial complex had held me captive. The bills were piling up. Since I would soon be on my way to a rehab center, that would be a reprieve from having to pay right away.

# Chapter 14

# Rehab: Relearning to Walk

The Good Samaritan PTs weren't accommodating. They were frustrated with me and punitive rather than motivational. I tried to comply with their requests, but the PT regimen wasn't working, mainly because I resisted their treatments due to the pain. That place was not in the business of physical rehabilitation. The time had come for me to move from the hospital and into a rehabilitation center.

I had hoped for Manor Care, a KP affiliate, in Boulder, which was less than a mile from Silver Sage Village, but there were no beds available. A day had passed, and still no room in Boulder.

Late afternoon on January 15, 2014, a nurse coaxed me out of bed. My legs and arms were so weak that I could barely hold myself up before I settled into a wheelchair. A Certified Nursing Assistant (CNA) pushed me to the back door, where an ambulance hauled me to Manor Care in Denver. I was surprised at how much muscle mass and strength I had lost during the month in the hospital.

Besides that, I was likely getting toward the end of my insurance benefit.

The EMT strapped me to a chair in the back of the ambulance and headed out of the hospital back door. I was very weak and flopped around like Bernie's corpse in *Weekend at Bernie's* (1989), about two insurance agents at a business retreat, where they find their lifeless boss. The two try to convince the other party-goers that Bernie is still alive by propping his dead body in chairs and animating him by flapping his limp arms and nodding his floppy head. I had little strength and was skinny after shedding 37 pounds.

I would have fit better into a child restraint seat. After all the bouncing around, I was too weak to hold myself up and slid out of the chair. The driver pulled into a parking lot on Quebec Street and repositioned my Raggedy Andy body.

The EMT rolled me to the Manor Care front door, where a smiling guy in a green sports coat and tie greeted me. We arrived at my room and reviewed a fancy notebook containing information about the services. Those included meal schedules, recreational activities, laundry service, and a coupon for a free haircut.

Compared to the hospital room, Manor Care was like a hotel with lovely carpeting and drapes that covered the windows. Just being there made me feel better. It took me a couple of days to get the hang of the place.

The days were monotonous. There was only so much rehab that the therapists could provide each day. Since I was so spindly and weak, my routine eased me in slowly with one hour-long session in the morning and another in the afternoon. The gentle approach was much better than the hospital PTs, who seemed like they wanted immediate results.

Even though the rooms were homier, when I wasn't rehabbing or eating, I would wheel myself into the hallway during the day, burn up a few hours, but there was still lots of downtime and boredom. I sat outside my door and watched as the nursing carts passed by, carrying the daily doses of medicine, while other patients walked around with their therapists, and staff dropped off meals to those who preferred delivery service.

I had my first meal in my room. That reminded me too much of the hospital, so I went to the dining room from then on out. The dietitians interspersed meals between sessions. All the tables were four-tops.

Wheelchairs were shorter than the regular chairs, which was good. My arms were shaking and my knees were weak, to quote Elvis. I had trouble lifting my food, and I had to shovel bites into my mouth. I wasn't usually a messy eater, but bibs, known as "clothes protectors," lay over the shoulders and didn't tie behind the neck. I imagine tie strings were a choking hazard.

A set menu was available. Choices were made by checking my options on a piece of paper. The breakfast menu consisted of general cafeteria cuisine, including scrambled rubber eggs, toast, and some type of meat. Most of the time, I went through the cereal buffet.

Lunch and dinner had the same meal service setup. I knew I was supposed to eat starchy foods covered in gravy because I needed to gain weight. I later learned that a special menu existed, which included items suitable for people with dietary restrictions, such as various sandwiches, hard-boiled eggs, and different salads.

A refrigerator also had drinks and ice cream, not on the menu. One drink option was a chocolate, vanilla, or strawberry-flavored nutritional protein liquid called Ensure, which had a pleasant taste.

Like similar institutions, the objective was to sustain life, not provide a gourmet experience. Outside food wasn't allowed. My friend, Amanda, smuggled in contraband, including Lays potato chips, Cheetos, and Snickers.

*******

The rehab center culture consisted of two cliques. The long-term people all knew each other because they all lived in the same area of the center. They ate together and were exclusive about who was allowed to sit with them. It seemed the long-termers were a lonely crowd. My impression was that some of those folks outlived their family and friends, and the only people they had for company were in the same situation.

I overheard the fellow who shooed me away from his dinner group, saying he needed to get a little stronger and would soon be heading home. On my way to treatment, I saw him sitting in the long-term living area hallway. He was a wishful thinker, and his optimism kept him moving forward. Rehab made me realize I didn't want to end up being the old guy at the club.

There was no reason a long-term resident at the end of their rope would want to waste time and energy getting to know a short-termer like me. I was 60 and one of the youngest people there. The radio in the dining area was tuned to a station that played 1940s Big Band-era music, which I didn't mind, since in my previous life, I had grown up listening to Glenn Miller and his orchestra playing the Hotel Pennsylvania in Manhattan.

I was amazed at the progress that I had made after seven days. When I first arrived, I couldn't get out of bed without first having a belt cinched around my spindly waist, and a CNA would assist me as I struggled to stand and plop myself in the wheelchair and head for the cafeteria.

My arms weren't strong enough to support myself in a walker. Before each of my sessions, the rehabilitation staff met to review each patient's case. The staff separated us into groups based on our daily progress.

The exercises included weights, stretching with large rubber bands, and workouts on treadmills and stationary bikes. I gained back a few pounds and became strong enough to use a walker and ambulate on my own with assistance.

I felt well enough to take in the whole Manor Care experience. A week before the Super Bowl, I wandered in my wheelchair to one of the other floors and joined an arts and crafts class. The activity involved decorating Styrofoam balls with paint and appliqués in the spirit of Broncos football. I painted mine orange with blue facial features.

It was hard for me to believe how miserable I was at the Good Samaritan Hospital.

# Chapter 15

# Emergency Surgery: Scrooge's Ghost

Before my release from the Good Samaritan Hospital, Scrooge's Ghost of Christmas Present visited me. He showed me how joyous and cheerful the outside world was, preparing for the holidays. Here in the hospital, things weren't going too well for me. I was nearly dead, and I was broke. Life had to get better. I wondered what my life would be like if and when I ever got up from the hospital bed.

The present reality was that when I was flat on my back, dealing with the KP member services office was the last thing on my mind. If I had been a more forward-thinking individual, in addition to needing a healthcare advocate, I would have appreciated working with a financial advocate who would have renewed my health insurance policy sooner, rather than when it was close to expiring.

"It's better for you to keep whatever coverage you have in place," the Ghost of the Present assured me. "If I let you go underwater, that would be bad for you and your insurance company. If you're not insured, that means the likelihood of you paying your medical bills is low. I don't want you to go bankrupt. I don't think you do either."

That was one of the many irons in the fire I had to pound out in December 2013. There was no way I wanted the world to know that I needed help with any of my commitments.

I still felt like crap and didn't have an appetite. My medical care team didn't seem to be trying very hard to figure out why, except to force Jell-O and applesauce down my throat.

*******

The hospitalist finally concluded that I had an ulcer that slowly leaked septic fluids into my abdominal cavity and ordered me into a second surgery.

The CNAs left some tiny sponges stuck to sticks, like lollipops. I dipped them in water to moisten my mouth, which reminded me of a scene from one of those "Bible" movies. A Jesus advocate dipped a wad of fabric stuck on a wooden rod into a bucket of water. A centurion raised it, and the King of Kings quenched His thirst by sucking out the moisture. Apparently, CNAs offer the sponges to patients on their last legs. I'm glad nobody mentioned that to me at the time.

Diana told me later that the doctors didn't give me much of a chance to make it through the procedure. No appetite and general mental indifference translated into "failure to thrive."

I woke up on December 29th after the surgery and looked up at my IV. A nurse had hooked me up to a bag filled with yellow, gunky pablum, which was gravity-fed to me through a Peripherally Inserted Central Catheter (PICC) line. The PICC bypassed my stomach and intestines while the ulcer patch healed.

The "food" caused me to lose weight and strength. After losing 37 pounds, I dropped to 107, my high school wrestling weight. When I later reviewed my medical record, the doctor classified me as anorexic.

I wondered why this random hospitalist was paying closer attention to me than my PCP. Hospitalists are a very well-kept secret. They provide more efficient care with the proliferation of insurance providers by eliminating the need for dozens of PCPs wandering the hospital, checking on patients.

With the rise of managed care, the number of patients admitted to hospitals increased significantly. The role of ER doctors no longer involves only dealing with immediate cases, but also includes hospitalization triage. As a result, there was a need for physicians who could provide timely and consistent care for hospitalized patients.

*******

While I was recuperating from the ulcer surgery, I received news from the University of Michigan pathology lab about my tissue samples snipped out of my lungs during the Video-Assisted Thoracic Surgery (VATS), the first procedure that I had within two weeks.

Go Wolverines!

The lab technicians determined that I had contracted Pneumocystis Pneumonia, caused by a fungus called Pneumocystis jirovecii. It is a rare but serious infection that primarily affects people who have weakened immune systems, such as those with HIV/AIDS or those undergoing chemotherapy. Similarly, I was susceptible because of a fragile immune system.

Then there are Out-of-Network costs. I was shocked to learn that I was billed full price for the pathology work. That was because the lab wasn't in the KP managed care network. The hospitalist should have given me options, but in the brevity of the moment, having to face surgery, the paperwork blurred in front of me, and my thoughts narrowed to survival. Medical advocates are so crucial during fast-moving situations like mine. I assumed everything was inside the system. Instead, I ended up paying out of pocket for lab work I hadn't even realized could fall outside the network.

After my diagnosis, the treatment that cleared out the fungus was simpler than I had imagined, with ordinary sulfa drugs. When working in Mexico, I always had a supply of over-the-counter Bactrim tablets with me for various intestinal bugs. I had no allergic reaction to Bactrim.

There's a concept known as "upcoding," as opposed to "downcoding," that occurs when hospitals bill Medicare for a more expensive procedure than the one that actually happened. It's like paying for a filet mignon and actually being served a hamburger steak. At first, I thought it sounded too brazen to be real. Then, my records indicated that I was allergic to Bactrim. The nurse brought a bad-tasting, orange-red-colored liquid alternative. I called my pharmacist friend Bill. He explained that it was new and not widely known.

I couldn't help but think that I was upcoded from Bactrim to this new drug.

I was getting back to health, but was very weak. The hospital physical therapists tried to get me up and about. Their efforts were counterproductive.

What Medicare sees on paper is a sanitized version of events. The real story lives in those gray spaces, where care and commerce intersect, and where patients are left to sort out the difference long after the stitches have healed.

For me, these weren't just billing quirks. They were reminders that our healthcare system isn't just about healing, but about navigating a maze of codes, networks, and clerical choices that can cost or save thousands of dollars. In that maze, patients stumble in the dark, trusting that someone on the other side has their best interests in mind. Sometimes they do. Sometimes they don't. When inconsistencies arise, it's possible that a data input technician is overworked, bored, or passive-aggressive.

I've come to judge American healthcare not based on the diagnoses, surgeries, or recoveries, but on the uncertainty that lingers long after the hospital gown is folded and put away. The scariest part is never knowing whether the next envelope in the mailbox will bring relief or raise my blood pressure.

Did I mention the morphine pump?

*******

The surgeries were piling up. Ten days earlier, on December 19th, I don't remember the exact time, but it was dark. A crew of Ninja staff wheeled in a portable X-ray machine. The X-ray technician cranked my hospital bed to an upright position and wedged a cartridge with a large film frame between my back and the mattress.

The VATS is minimally invasive, but it resulted in a bunch of holes punched into my lungs. Fluids accumulated around all the wounds and drained into a bucket beside my bed. That was another painful experience.

The Ghost of Christmases Yet to Come visited Scrooge in a nightmare. The ghost had shown him how to recognize and reverse his self-centered ways, as he omnisciently watched how his friends and family would treat him after his death.

Two weeks before, Scrooge's Ghost of the Future visited me when I had become more intimately acquainted with the healthcare system than I had ever imagined. I had unfounded optimism about my short-term prospects and felt pretty good when the ER staff administered fluids to me through an IV. Being the eternal optimist, I was sure I'd be out by Christmas. That was wishful thinking.

What I learned about myself while in the hospital was life-changing, but I don't recommend it as the best way to lose weight.

I built strong relationships with the hospital caregivers and tip my hat to healthcare workers in the trenches, namely nurses and Certified Nursing Assistants (CNAs). The healthcare world wouldn't turn without them.

I couldn't walk or stand up, and it was excruciatingly painful when I tried. I developed bedsores and couldn't wipe my butt. Luckily, nurses and CNAs were there to meet my every need, particularly when I felt bummed out.

One night, I dreamt of suddenly standing up and getting around in a walker. The room was sideways, like inside the Space Shuttle, where I climbed around on the walls using ladders. I woke up terrified in a dark room by myself. I kept pushing the call button, but nobody came. It was a very helpless feeling. A nurse finally showed up, and I yelled at her for not being at her post, which was a big overreaction. I expected a certain level of service, which apparently was unavailable in the middle of the night.

That lack of support from the hospital staff raised another big topic: self-advocacy. I was complacent, mostly because I was mentally and physically out of it and couldn't advocate for myself as much as I should have.

*******

My winter holiday celebrations, as an adult, have been a new experience every year. Being in the hospital for Christmas 2013, along with the second-tier medical staff on duty, would be the most different Christmas of my life, but not surprising. I thought I'd be home by Christmas.

A few days earlier, Diana had to call 911 on December 16th. The cops, a fire truck, and an ambulance all pulled up with lights flashing and drove me to the Good Samaritan Hospital, located 20 miles away in Lafayette. The check-in desk immediately admitted me to the ER, and a nurse ordered me into the Intensive Care Unit (ICU) under the care of a hospitalist.

Hospitalists are generally internal medicine doctors who take over where the ER doctor left off. They tend to hospitalized patients by coordinating care with the patient's PCP and specialists. Hospitalists order tests and medications, and work closely with other providers, ensuring they are available 24 hours a day.

The moment my head hit the ICU pillow, it was a huge relief. My breathing was constrained when the ICU nurse outfitted me with a device that forced more air into my lungs. I wasn't sick enough to have a ventilator tube stuck down my windpipe. I could sleep through just about anything, but that was noisy.

The day before was frustrating. I was so sick that Diana drove me to the hospital and dropped me off. She returned to Boulder to pack a bag for me. The thought was that I would be admitted to the hospital that night. I went through ER triage but was released. I don't know what he was thinking since his notes from that night indicated I had sepsis.

Diana was beside herself. She asked my neighbor, Jim, across the sidewalk, to pick me up from the hospital. I returned home from a quick trip to the ER just in time for the SSV community holiday party, which followed the Sunday potluck dinner. The fare was my favorite: turkey and roast beef with all the trimmings, but those dishes weren't appetizing. I barely touched my plate. I went home after dinner and missed the white elephant gift exchange.

I made it to bed, woke up the next day, got dressed, and plopped on the couch.

So over two days, I came, left, and then went back to stay in the hospital. Society had pounded Superman's American Way into my head since the day I popped out of the womb in my first life, and I ignored my illness. You know, faster than a speeding bullet, more powerful than a locomotive, able to leap tall buildings in a single bound, strong is better than weak, I don't need your help, I'm a rugged individual.

There was no way I was going to admit that I would be unable to complete my appointed tasks, which included reapplying for my insurance coverage. I learned that staying out of the healthcare system was better than entering the endless health-scare loop.

If I only had a choice.

Chapter 16

# Ask for Help: Plan for the Unexpected

I won't say that my life flashed before my eyes when the ambulance hauled me off from my Silver Sage Village front porch in December 2013, but I had the mistaken impression that my illness was minor and I'd be home in no time, and dealing with my KP insurance would be no big deal.

It was a rude awakening.

I could have benefited from advocates to clear the extra ambulance ride, alternative drugs, and numerous lab tests that my high-deductible plan didn't cover. I thought I could do that myself.

Not.

The hospital cut me some slack and delayed payments, but some of the other vendors did not. The hospital offered a grant program to defray some of the costs. I was low-income, but not low enough to qualify for assistance.

Luckily, I had a reluctant but dedicated healthcare advocate and partner in crime, Diana, who paid attention to the hospital service. She grew weary of dealing with doctors and nurses who had more than just my case on their clipboards and asked a couple of her friends to help.

**99**

Doctors tend to many patients and support people who do the best they can to keep track of everyone recuperating from minor surgeries, illnesses, and those on their deathbeds, like me.

"Hmm, I wonder how that Alan is doing?" I doubt any of them went home wondering about me during a pregnant pause while sitting around the dinner table.

Unless you pay attention or have someone else as a second set of eyes and ears, you're pretty much on your own, and that was a problem for me, considering I was out of it on drugs.

Reading my healthcare summary, my prognosis was at best pessimistic. I was in denial that anything was wrong with me. I should have gone to the ER much sooner than I did. Based on the level of care I received when I visited the ER the first time, the results may not have been any better, except for saving one round-trip.

Once I was out of the ICU, I intended to do some video editing and complete some paperwork. My computer bag sat unopened the entire time. I was in no frame of mind to do anything functional except watch endless *reruns of Pawn Stars* and *Law & Order: SVU*. It was also college football bowl season. I didn't know chicken companies sponsored so many post-season games. There must be big money in fowl taste.

I'd say that most Americans, including me, struggle with asking for help. I wasn't very good at that life skill until helplessness shocked me into undoing my hubris.

That line worked for a while until project due dates crept closer and closer. A few friends visited me in the hospital with cards and flowers to ask if I was well enough to fulfill my obligations.

I coordinate video production for the BIFF every year. Before hitting the wall, I started organizing that in November by speaking to one of the University of Colorado's TV news production classes. Since I convinced myself I'd be back on my feet by Christmas, I had nothing to worry about. It soon became apparent that I would be unable to fulfill that obligation.

In addition to the BIFF gig, the State of Wyoming Arts Council had contracted me to produce video tributes for Governor Matt Mead's art award recipients. Luckily, my production pal, Michael, agreed to help out, brave Wyoming winter roads, and do the job.

My estranged friend coordinated the Wyoming artist tribute schedule with Michael. She was also skilled with finances and completed the accounting and final report for the *Mahjong and the West* Wyoming film incentive production.

While I didn't mind parting with the funds to pay my friends to complete these projects, those expenses were unplanned. I'm now a believer in the division of labor. Any job I undertake now has a budget allocated for additional contractors to complete specific tasks.

*******

This hospital stay was the first time I was truly helpless, and my survival was in the hands of strangers. Some of the faces became familiar from one shift to the next, but I mainly learned to identify the worker types by the color of their uniforms. A 2015 study showed that nearly 70 percent of patients had difficulty identifying hospital staff. As I recall, my doctors wore white lab jackets. I didn't see my doctor before surgery.

CNAs in maroon scrubs were at the bottom of the healthcare industrial complex and tirelessly turned me over so I would avoid bedsores. They changed the bed linens and wiped my butt.

Then there were the underpaid nurses in dark blue scrubs who came into the room at all hours to take my temperature and change my bandages. Some could manage the tests in the dark. Others flipped on the lights, which was very annoying.

"I just like helping people, no matter what," a nurse responded after I asked about her job. "It gives me a good feeling knowing I helped someone get better."

She was quite the optimist, considering everyone on the staff knows how all the patients are doing at any given moment, and that's generally pretty miserable at best. When I was released, they did it all over and over again and again for the next group of sick strangers.

On some days, the hallways would be bustling with people coming and going, and chatter would fill the waiting areas. Then the next day, it would be silent. I presumed it was because the visitors who gathered to be with their soon-to-be departed friend or family member had fulfilled their "quality time" obligations.

"We just wanted to stop by and spend a few minutes of quality time with you." I'd rather have my last association with my friends and family when I'm still coherent and can get around without a walker or wheelchair.

"Quality time? Where were you BEFORE my eyes had glazed over from this morphine pump, and I could still remember your name?" is what I'd be thinking in my drug-induced coma.

I also thought that if I were on my deathbed, I would recount the experience in a journal. Being on drugs and totally out of it, writing a story based on my experience was the last thing on my mind. Being helpless and sick is hard work if you plan to tell your end-of-life story from a hospital bed. Be sure you have a good intern or two, and pay them!

I found solace when a lullaby played at all hours. That signaled a birth. Anecdotally, I noted that there were more births than deaths. The hospital was a sign that the world strives for equilibrium. My hunch was right. There are about 17 percent more births than deaths.

*******

Not only are health care advocates necessary, but also financial advocates who can question what your doctors and hospital order. In hindsight, I was in no position to reapply for a new health insurance policy when I was on drugs. Not only did I have a high-deductible plan in 2013, but I also had a new high-deductible plan for the following year. I had no idea what my new monthly premium would be.

# Chapter 17

# Obamacare: Two Big Deductibles

If you have ever had to prove you're poor, it's a very demeaning and oppressive process. That was me when I was mentally out of it in the hospital. I didn't predict my health emergency, but I did the best I could with the information I had at the time. Towards the end of 2013, like every year, I received an annual letter reminding me that my policy would expire and that I would need to renew my enrollment. KP wrote that I had the opportunity to sign up for a KP policy provided through the Affordable Care Act (ACA or Obamacare) or, since I had coverage before Obamacare went into effect, my current policy was, for the time being, "grandfathered," meaning that if it didn't meet the basic ACA coverage criteria, it would still be good.

As a quick primer, the U.S. Congress approved Obama's healthcare system overhaul. He signed the bill into law on March 23, 2010. After two years, the bureaucracy had finally caught up.

It took a few years, but ACA set up centralized health insurance exchanges where users not covered by their employer, the Veterans Administration, Medicaid, Medicare, or some other program could sign up for health insurance.

Obamacare changed the rules. Medicaid would now cover all adults under 65 who earn up to 138% of the federal poverty level, regardless of their family status or disability. In theory, that expansion cracked open the door for millions of people like me who didn't always fit neatly into the old categories. There were provisions, such as not being denied coverage for pre-existing conditions and allowing young people to be covered under their parents' policies until they were 26 years old.

Then politics got in the way. The Supreme Court said states didn't have to expand Medicaid. That meant access to healthcare became a matter of geography. The difference between being poor in Colorado or being poor in Wyoming could decide whether you got care at all.

Medicaid has been around a long time. It was born in 1965, alongside Medicare, as part of Lyndon Johnson's Great Society. In those early decades, it wasn't meant for everyone. It only covered certain groups, including poor children, pregnant women, some parents, people with disabilities, and seniors who needed long-term care. If you didn't fit into one of those categories, you were out of luck.

At the time, KP could cancel my policy if it didn't meet the ACA minimum standards for coverage. If I kept or changed my current coverage, there would be no repercussions from any pre-existing conditions I had or may develop. I also qualified for tax credits. I reviewed the options and learned that all the Obamacare plans were less expensive, met or exceeded the minimum standards, and were better than the one I had.

I had heard that when the ACA was in its infancy, KP notified several thousand individual policyholders by letter that their policies had been canceled because the coverage didn't meet the minimum ACA requirements. The ACA naysayers sought out stories about self-employed individuals who had their policies nixed.

What kind of coverage would that have been, like a barbecue grill warranty at Walmart? What was the big deal? As long as I worked at a job or was self-employed, I had to accept or reject a new plan for the upcoming year, which generally cost more for the same coverage. I seldom went to the doctor and always chose to increase my deductible to keep the monthly premiums reasonable.

Obama caused a few problems when he said that people would be able to keep their PCPs. That wasn't always true if a person changed policies and a favorite doctor was no longer in the network. He could have said that if a PCP was the most important consideration, they should follow the doctor to the new network and change insurance companies.

Before Obamacare, there was no national healthcare exchange. Instead, private ones offered packaged deals, similar to a travel agency.

As a pioneer, in October 2013, my illness hadn't gotten any better. I set up an account on the Connect for Colorado Health, the ACA insurance exchange. The online insurance exchange itself was clunky and unreliable in those first months. Millions of people, myself included, struggled with broken links, error messages, and endless wait times. The federal system crashed under the load. State exchanges weren't much better. I got caught up in that mess, too, and the frustration was nationwide. The failures were so public that Kathleen Sebelius, the Secretary of Health and Human Services at the time, ended up resigning under political and public pressure.

Much to my surprise, the lower deductible policies, graded as Silver, Gold, and Platinum, proved to be more expensive. I worked directly with KP, and they approved a better plan at a lower price. Although it was still expensive, the income-based tax credits would help lower the costs. My policy would expire at the end of 2013, and if I had kept it, the price would have doubled.

The reason high-deductible plans became so common on the exchanges is simple. They were the cheapest way to meet the ACA's new coverage requirements. Insurers were required to include a basic set of benefits in every plan, regardless of the plan's cost. To keep monthly premiums affordable for lower-income individuals, and to prevent insurers from withdrawing from the exchanges, particularly in rural states, the trade-off was higher deductibles. Premiums remained manageable, but patients had to pay more out of pocket before the coverage took effect. For someone who stayed healthy most of the year, the math worked, but for anyone with a major medical crisis, it could mean financial devastation.

The higher premium price was a self-employment cost and increased every year. I was no longer on Medicare, and the premiums of my individual policy had decreased as I became younger.

The prices were based on actuarial tables that showed low-income and older individuals tended to have more extensive health problems than the general population, which is why a diverse group of people is necessary for the risk pool. My "low-end" policy price was considerably less with the tax credits applied. In my case:

**-ACA saved me a few bucks** on premiums and lots of bucks on prescriptions.

**-ACA gave me peace of mind** about the future because my policy wouldn't get canceled.

**-ACA covered a whole bunch of people** who theoretically would stop relying on the ER doctor as their PCP, which, in the long run, kept my premiums lower by placing them and their risk in a separate pool of patients and not in mine.

I think the national healthcare exchanges were good if you were eligible for tax credits and didn't already have coverage. Most people had coverage when the ACA went into effect, and if you do, I suggest sticking with your carrier. If you're in the market or curious about your options, consider exploring a public or private online healthcare exchange in your home area. Like all other internet commerce, be careful!

Initially, I was "double-covered" by my existing and new ACA policy because I didn't entirely trust the new system. I finally gained confidence and canceled my other, higher-deductible plan. I didn't qualify for Medicaid this time. My relationship with Medicaid has always been like a seesaw I could never quite balance. Sometimes I qualified, sometimes I didn't. It depended on my income, my zip code, and rules I barely understood. Obamacare established "dual eligibility" for individuals aged 65 and older who are enrolled in both Medicare and Medicaid. Medicare pays for the basics, Medicaid fills in some of the gaps, and I still feel like I need a lawyer to explain the paperwork.

Don't get seriously sick at the end of the year. I had two big deductible amounts. One was at the end of 2013, the other at the beginning of 2014, meaning I had $16,000 out-of-pocket costs that I had to cover before my insurance benefit picked up the slack. It didn't help that I'd not been making any money and had a cash flow problem.

# Chapter 18

# High Stress: When My Body Said 'No'

I had finally resolved my insurance renewal, but the bill collectors continued to pound on my door. I had to keep the cameras rolling to generate any income to stave them off.

In August, my good friends, Bob and Jill, hired me to document their daughter, Jessica's, June wedding in Cheyenne. I only do weddings for people I know. Another drive, another time, lugging around a set of cameras and memory cards, another promise to be fully present while my mind was scattered across a half dozen unfinished projects. Smiles, vows, champagne flutes, the first dance. I captured it all, but under the surface, I was fraying. I hired a fellow video guy to help me schlep things around.

It would be my body's way of saying: enough.

*******

On top of it all, the financial stress added to my physical and emotional exhaustion. Dr. Lookner referred me to a pulmonologist, Dr. Kinnard. I don't know how I ended up in the hospital, as my medical record has no documentation, but I assume Dr. Kinnard directly admitted me. He ordered high doses of intravenous steroids.

After I checked in, he gave me the option of having Video Assisted Thoracoscopic Surgery (VATS), which entailed extracting multiple biopsy samples from different places in my lungs under full anesthesia, or having a probe crammed down my trachea. I chose the latter.

That stay was the longest I'd been in the hospital, and very leisurely. I was able to dress in street clothes even though a nurse tethered me to a rally pack filled with saline and Prednisone. There was a food menu with lots of choices. I ate better than usual.

The probe results didn't find anything out of the ordinary, and Kinnard released me on August 19th. The steroid solution did its job. After being released, I felt pretty good, but soon I was run down, my finger joints began to burn, and my saliva was thick and stringy. I consulted Dr. Google, and my self-diagnosis was arthritis and Sjogren's (SHOW-greens) Syndrome. The soonest I could get a rheumatology appointment was at the KP medical offices in Denver.

Sure enough, the rheumatologist determined I had developed an autoimmune condition. Viral infections can trigger Sjogren's, which accompanies rheumatoid arthritis (RA). My immune system began producing antibodies that attacked a layer of cells called the synovium, releasing harmful chemicals that, if left untreated, would damage my bones, cartilage, tendons, and ligaments.

Why RA occurs in some people and not in others is unknown, but my case is consistent with the viral infection and the hereditary theories. RA attacks several joints at once. I had several aching fingers, my right wrist, and elbow. My joint linings were inflamed and painful. My balance wasn't impaired, nor had my hands become deformed, because I decided to be proactive and managed my condition with medicine that slowed the disease progression and acupuncture to reduce pain.

I made an appointment with Dr. Hagen, a rheumatologist who was nearby at the Rock Creek Clinic in Lafayette. He prescribed Plaquenil, the debunked COVID-19 treatment, to decrease my joint pain and swelling and reduce the risk of long-term disability.

I shouldn't have ignored the subtle sign that I had beaten my immune system to a pulp from working too much. I thrived in stressful situations. Rather than slow down, I sped up, which caused my immune system to produce anti-inflammatory responses that included contracting deadly infections.

Including the wedding, what brought all this on was self-inflicted and stemmed from trying to catch up by taking on too much in too short a time. My video production work was hand-to-mouth, meaning if the cameras weren't rolling, money didn't flow into my wallet. Beginning three months earlier, I traveled extensively during the summer of 2013 and didn't mind driving out of Colorado because my KP policy covered emergencies outside its coverage area.

One significant downside of an HMO is that its closed network is typically limited to a specific geographic region. KP has a physical presence in a few states. If I needed emergency services, a co-pay would cover those situations.

*******

Diana wanted to visit her family in Boston. On the way, we stopped in New York City and stayed with my Hastings College frat brother, Tom. The trip had already been a whirlwind, flying out of Denver, straight into New York chaos. The outing was supposed to be a little jolt of fun before I headed back West.

I should have known something was wrong when I was rumbling up and down on a rickety old wooden rollercoaster in Brooklyn, New York. Riding the Cyclone at Coney Island, with the Atlantic in the distance, was on the top of my bucket list. While the car momentarily paused at the apex, my scalp gave a strange twinge, like a hot sting. I dismissed it as the wind or the rush of nerves before the drop.

I thought about what might happen if there was an accident on top of the Cyclone, just in time to careen down the last steep straightaway to the bottom of the ride.

A crash would be the least of my worries.

It's not that I was a roller coaster buff, but riding the Cyclone was on my bucket list. After stepping out of the fire engine red car, I felt another pinpoint twinge on my left scalp. I didn't think anything of it and attributed it to my unsteady dizziness from the raucous ride.

I received a phone call while on the rickety wooden coaster, which foreshadowed me nearly kicking the bucket. It was a movie director named Joe. I returned the call when I stepped out of the red roller coaster car at the end of the big thrill ride.

He asked if I could do some pre-production work on the *Mahjong* project, which would be shooting in and around Jackson and Jackson Hole, Wyoming, south of Yellowstone Park, later in the summer.

"Can I get back to you?" I asked while getting reoriented with the ground. That afternoon, we spoke again, and I agreed to be part of the production, but only after I had completed the series of video profiles of artists around Wyoming for the Wyoming Arts Council.

*******

There wasn't much breathing space waiting for me. I landed back in Denver, barely had time to unpack before I was packing again. My physical and emotional exhaustion had its own itinerary. It had been riding shotgun the whole time.

I thought I could outrun the stress from my whirlwind drive from Boulder to Jackson, Cody, Tensleep, Casper, and back to Boulder to interview people for the Wyoming Arts Council artist tribute videos. It was a long and meandering drive, the kind where audiobooks and highway signs blur into one another. Rehearsing my questions, I was silently running on gas station coffee and adrenaline.

I spent the night at the rustic Antler Hotel, my favorite place to stay in Jackson. The following morning, I interviewed a 3-D artist who created sculptures out of vinyl car seat upholstery material that zipped up into various shapes. I then spoke with a painter to complete the task before facing another four-hour drive to Cody.

Rooms in Cody were expensive and scarce after Yellowstone National Park had opened in May. I found a log cabin-like room at the Cowboy Village. My scalp pain was the precursor to a full-blown case of herpes zoster, aka shingles.

Overnight, the tingling transformed into visible blisters and sores. The KP advice service suggested I get checked out at a local urgent care facility. It was June 8th when the doctor diagnosed me with shingles. Shingles typically manifests as a band of blisters covering the left side of the torso. My case wrapped around the left side of my scalp and forehead. The Nurse Practitioner prescribed an antiviral pill called acyclovir, which is the most effective if taken within a few hours of the first symptoms.

"Shingles" has old linguistic roots. The name originates from the Latin word *cingulum*, meaning belt or girdle, through the French word *cingles*. Doctors noticed the rash often appears in a belt-like strip around one side of the torso, following the path of a nerve. Historically, shingles was also called zoster from the Greek *zōstēr*, also meaning "belt" or "girdle," which is why the medical name is *herpes zoster*.

It took me a while to put two and two together that chickenpox would lead to shingles later in life. Was it better to get chickenpox as a kid? Now that I think about it, I should have taken my chances. The disease is undeniably harsher in adults. I ran a high fever, was lethargic, and the rash spread more severely.

Mom didn't know the long shadow cast by her decision to take me to the neighborhood chickenpox party. In her 1920s and 1930s world, children contracted chickenpox. It was as ordinary as the common cold, something every parent expected to endure in the household. Doctors treated it with oatmeal baths, powders, and patience. There was no mention of vaccines, nor was there any notion that scientists might one day link shingles in old age to that itchy childhood rash.

Shingles had been striking adults all along, but few made the connection. In earlier times, life was shorter. A man in his 50s might already have been considered old, and if he broke out in a painful rash along his side or scalp, doctors might have dismissed his condition as random pain or bad luck. Families whispered about it in kitchens, neighbors noticed a band of blisters on a torso, but no one tied it back to a childhood disease. Shingles was just another burden of age.

Only in the mid-20th century did researchers prove that the same virus causes chickenpox and shingles. By the 1980s, doctors began prescribing antiviral medications like acyclovir, although not as widely as they are today, and certainly not as the go-to treatment most doctors recognize now.

The hitch was that I could get my acyclovir prescription covered by KP, but only if they mailed the pills to me. I had to pay full price at the local pharmacy. Compared to $3.50, the retail price was $25. I waited too long to take the pills, so the medicine was ineffective.

Chickenpox is one disease that I should have dodged as a kid. Shingles emerged decades later. I was one of the unlucky 15 percent with lingering PHN that remained after the blisters had healed. It was definitely a lot more painful than chicken-pox.

Medical experts recommend that old guys like me get the shingles vaccine at age 60, which I didn't. The shingles out-break was the start of a long and miserable summer.

I traveled too much, was overworked, and rode too many roller coasters. Turning 60 and having an immunodeficiency were likely what brought about my shingles attack. The vari-cella-zoster virus causes the adult flare-up, which results in a painful rash. It's the same virus that causes chicken pox.

If you had chickenpox as a kid, the virus remains in your body as long as you're alive.

My health became progressively worse. The next stop was in Tensleep to interview an accomplished banjo player, Jalan Crossland. Governor Matt Mead awarded Jalan one of his an-nual art awards. After a scenic drive over the Big Horn Moun-tains to Buffalo, I interviewed a guy who gave a testimonial about Jalan. That night should have been a relaxing stay at the historic Occidental Hotel. It was anything but.

*******

My health had gotten worse. I made two drives to help with *Mahjong* in Jackson. I was so lethargic and weak that the pro-ducers sent me back to Boulder. My primary function was to manage expenses and oversee payroll remotely from my office.

I planned to live in Jackson for a month or two, monitoring the *Mahjong* movie production. I dragged around and could barely walk, let alone struggle up staircases, lugging around camera equipment. I was in Jackson twice before the produc-tion team banished me back to Boulder. I had to perform much of my administrative work from my Boulder office, which included cutting the payroll for the cast and crew.

After the movie wrapped, there were the hassles of dealing with bogus unemployment claims. I compiled receipts for expenses incurred during the production for submittal to the Wyoming Film Incentive program for reimbursement.

My plate was full, but I offered to take on the work and eventually qualify the movie for the Wyoming Film Office's financial incentive aspect of the movie production. Many state governments offer rebates or grants to out-of-state productions that film, produce, or advertise within their state. The idea was to create a few local jobs and retail sales.

The main film incentive in a sparsely populated state like Wyoming is the incredible scenery in and around Jackson. The liabilities are many. Productions compete with tourists. The most accessible season in Wyoming is summer. There were few hotel rooms and even fewer bed and breakfast places available. For the few coveted vacancies, the room-night costs were out of this world.

As for job creation, we transported all the principal crew, including the director, lighting and sound personnel, the cinematographer, lens puller, and actors, from out of state. We hired the gaffer (electrical services) truck from California.

The only local jobs available were a few positions for background actors and production assistants. Compounding the situation was Jackson's isolation. There is an airport that shuttles primarily tourists. Flights weren't frequent, and rental cars were few.

I enjoyed dealing with production limitations, and bridging them with creative problem-solving was a positive challenge. These were stressful and, in retrospect, not worth the pittance I earned and the health problems that followed.

"The show must go on. I can't be sick," I thought. The next few months were more financially destabilizing for me than when I first relocated to Colorado. I had dropped out of the mainstream economy and figured I could do my work from anywhere, even being flat on my back. It wasn't like I had a real job and could rely on vacation and sick days while being paid my salary.

I made an appointment to see Dr. Lookner. He knew something was wrong with me, but couldn't do much except help with remediation and make referrals. My best hope was to go to the ER. I didn't go because I'm one who thought that ERs and ambulances should be reserved for people in car crashes or dying from a heart attack, not for sick people who could transport themselves and were tired.

I wasn't as old as I was, and my health improved as my body grew younger, but I still had to contend with those recommended nuisance prevention measures, like colonoscopies.

# Chapter 19

# Fantastic Voyage: My First Colonoscopy

Cohousing has neighborly support built into the social contract. My age was progressing toward youth. When I was 58, my neighbor Henry and I were having a conversation on the back porch. Our small talk soon transitioned to uneasiness about my first colonoscopy. I was getting emails from KP that I was overdue for the cancer-detecting test, which wasn't an around-the-water-cooler topic in other circles.

I didn't have a family history of colorectal cancer and had been putting off the procedure for several years, and what to expect was a big mystery. Cost wasn't a factor because my KP policy covered preventative treatments. This story may be TMI, but I think part of my fear came from a reluctance to talk about my butt.

"You're out during the whole thing," Henry advised. "If you need some support, I'll give you a ride to the hospital."

I wasn't thrilled about being anesthetized and having a guided video tour of my large intestine taken by a colonoscope inserted through the rectum. At that time, medical experts recommended that the age range for a colonoscopy was 50 to 75 years old.

Then there was the prep. After I made the appointment at KP, the mail-order pharmacy sent me a list of instructions on how to clean out my digestive tract before the procedure. The recipe called for taking a few Dulcolax tablets and chasing them with a slurry of Gatorade and Miralax. I planned it out so I wouldn't have to be up at all hours of the night and spend the day running back and forth to the pot. That was a good thing since I woke up rested the next day.

I had some experience with laxatives while on the high school wrestling team. For me to make weight, I took mild diuretics and laxatives to shed water. That wasn't the healthiest choice for a 16-year-old, but if I wanted a place on the team, that was the price I paid.

Three days before the colonoscopy, the KP gastrointestinal doctor instructed me to abstain from anything that might get caught in my intestinal nooks and crannies, such as raw fruits and vegetables, nuts, and corn. On the day of the procedure, the instructions were to go directly to the hospital and refrain from eating or drinking anything. Henry was my designated driver. He was a sympathetic soul because he was diagnosed with precancer after his most recent colonoscopy and had several feet of his intestine removed as a precaution.

I wasn't particularly nervous, but on the drive to the hospital, Henry explained what to expect and assured me that it wasn't anything to worry about. I had never been under full anesthesia before, which was my biggest unknown.

I checked in while Henry sat in the waiting room. When the attendant called my name, Henry wished me well, folded up his newspaper, and wandered to the cafeteria for a cup of coffee.

The pre-operation space was crammed wall-to-wall with patients awaiting their turn. The nurse came in and got me situated.

"Do you want 'mild' or 'out?'" The nurse gave me a choice about how much anesthetic I wanted. I chose mild and remembered the CNA wheeling me into the operating room, but I woke up before the gastroenterologist began his magic.

"Are you okay?" The doctor wanted to know if I needed more anesthesia. "You're welcome to watch."

I opted to stay awake and observe the procedure on a closed-circuit TV monitor. When the doctor inserted the colonoscope, I could feel the tube making its way through my abdomen, which was a strange sensation.

The colonoscopy reminded me of a science fiction movie called *Fantastic Voyage* (1966). A submarine crew, including the late Raquel Welch, is miniaturized and injected into the body of a spy. The camera followed the tiny crew as it traveled through a blood vessel to remove a blood clot. The camera led the way and took me on a journey through my innards.

My procedure didn't take an hour. The doctor told me I could request a copy of the video. I haven't yet taken him up on the offer.

I met Henry in the waiting area. We had an uneventful drive back to Boulder, although he was surprised that I was awake through the procedure.

*******

Colonoscopies must be effective because the rate of colorectal cancer has dropped dramatically since 1992, according to the National Cancer Institute.

Starting when we are kids, the culture teaches us that anything having to do with our heinies is not socially acceptable. There isn't even one common polite term. I searched for slang in the Urban Dictionary: coochie, bum, butt, and rear end. Then there are the vulgar monikers that were blocked out. I quit counting after "arse."

Dr. William I. Wolff and Dr. Hiromi Shinya developed the colonoscopy procedure in 1969, which is known today. Before they created a better colonoscope, there were war stories about how it didn't quite make the tight corners and punctured the intestinal lining, causing sepsis and death.

Colonoscopies became more convenient after Wolff and Shinya developed a combination camera and polyp-removing device. Previously, patients would have to schedule a second appointment to have any abnormalities removed.

Not having to come back a second time was a big selling point for me.

The two pooper pioneers published what experts consider to be the essential article about their revolutionary approach in the Seminars in Colon and Rectal Surgery journal. The editors in 1999 named that article "one of the most important of the 20th century." It's also good to know that many experts are considering this health issue.

*******

A few days later, I received an email from KP that said I had the guts of a 30-year-old and wouldn't need to get another colonoscopy for 10 years. If any polyps are found and removed, a five-year plan is in place. I laughed and admitted I had a competitive edge since the 1970s. Every morning, I stirred a spoonful of Metamucil into a glass of water and downed it like a ritual. It wasn't fancy medicine or some exotic tonic, just orange-flavored powder that turned into a pulpy gel.

I didn't really think about it at the time, but that daily spoonful was doing quiet, invisible work. The psyllium husk in Metamucil is a soluble fiber. It soaks up water and bulks out like a sponge, making the daily trip to the bathroom less of a battle. That little ritual meant I wasn't straining, and my colon wasn't getting the wear and tear that shows up in people my age.

There was another hidden trick. The fiber nourishes the beneficial bacteria that live down there in the dark. They thrive on it, turning it into fuel that protects the colon walls. You don't see it, you don't feel it, but the doctors can. The lining stays calmer, smoother, and younger.

On top of that, Metamucil gave the impression of tidiness. The colonoscopy camera likes a clean stage, and the fiber helped sweep things along, so there wasn't as much lingering debris. The doctor could see what he needed to see, and what he saw looked young and healthy.

I cheated, but it was the kind of cheating that came from listening to my body and giving it a simple daily habit. A spoonful of powder and a glass of water was my secret weapon.

# Chapter 20

# Work Leads Nowhere: Jobs and Gigs

S ilver Sage Village kicked me out when I was 50, as I continued on my youthful spiral. I no longer met the community's age criteria. Compounding my un-aging, I was too healthy, which I attribute to psyllium.

I found myself progressing toward young adulthood with a healthy colon at various workplaces. Working a regular job was a drag, but the daily grind was a necessary evil for the sake of employee benefits. Unlike countries much older than the United States, working-age Americans have had to rely on the private sector to provide health insurance.

The average American will hold 12 jobs over their lifetime. I've had seven. My dad worked for one employer, Coca-Cola, for 40 years before retiring. The parent owner sold Dad's local company during the 1990s, a period of intense corporate mergers and acquisitions. It wasn't until then that he had health insurance benefits.

The first few years of the 21st century were a challenging time. There were plenty of jobs, but none for a Colorado newbie. Since I had lived this life before, I should have taken notice.

Bidding on consulting contracts became tiring. My gig work was detrimental because, although I managed several contracts, employers viewed it as a liability. "Why would we hire a 'job-hopper? You only keep jobs for a few weeks or months," an interviewer would ask when I applied for regular jobs.

"Would you rather have a worker who is efficient and completes work quickly or an employee who just puts in the time and ends up costing you money?" was my typical response. Prospective bosses weren't interested in an independent sort because the 9 to 5 life was all they knew, and they couldn't imagine hiring someone who could keep multiple balls in the air.

*******

Getting work is a numbers game. I eventually had two real jobs.

A domestic violence legal advocacy organization laid me off. Just when my unemployment benefits were about to expire, a positive youth development organization hired me to develop a donor base.

One foundation grant funded the group, but it would soon run out of money. I delayed my start date for a week because my father died at DePaul Hospital.

When I returned for my first day of work, I discovered that the woman who had hired me had resigned and taken a new job with the City of Denver. Two years later, the organization no longer required my services. The layoff was a result of conflicts with my new boss over fundraising priorities, and I was hired too late to significantly reconfigure their business cash flow cycle. Luckily, I had maintained my individual health insurance policy from when I lost my job at the domestic violence organization.

I was lucky to land a job before September 11, 2001. A domestic violence prevention nonprofit hired me to raise money and write grants. After the terrorist attack in New York City, donor behavior changed to funding first responder assistance organizations and the Red Cross.

I sensed potential problems ahead. I retained my sole proprietorship, Environmental and Cultural Organization Systems (ECOS), and bid on side contracts to hedge against the volatile post-9/11 economy.

As bad luck would have it, two years later, though, the woman who hired me retired. My new boss cut my hours and eventually laid me off in 2003.

Rather than retain my employer-provided insurance, through the Consolidated Omnibus Budget Reconciliation Act of 1986 (COBRA) benefits, I kept up my high-deductible KP individual policy as a hedge against layoffs.

The COBRA allows laid-off employees to pay the monthly insurance premiums from their previous employer's coverage and maintain their policy. COBRA gave me an appreciation for the value of employer-provided health insurance. The premiums would have taken a big chunk out of my severance money. Luckily, as I became younger, the insurance premium prices decreased because, on average, elders aren't as healthy as younger individuals.

COBRA required businesses to offer healthcare benefits to employees who leave the company voluntarily or involuntarily at the same price for up to eighteen months of coverage

The domestic violence prevention work was personally fulfilling. Everyone, at some point in their lives, should work for a feminist organization.

*******

I applied for jobs to maintain my unemployment benefits, but I also continued my entrepreneurial pursuits and learned new skills at the local community TV station. I was also in grad school at the University of Colorado in Denver, ironically studying nonprofit management and domestic violence prevention.

For most people, there was little to no transition in health insurance policies if they were covered on the job or through another federal or state program. Shortly after the ACA became law, the U.S. population, employers provided health insurance benefits to 49 percent of the national workforce, and other forms of insurance covered 43 percent. The number of people benefiting from Obamacare was eight percent, including self-employed starving artists like me.

When I had a real job, I was surprised to learn that my policy covered me for maternity care as a single guy in my group plan. I understood why, after it was explained to me, that spreading the risk required me to help cover my colleagues who had families or might want to start one. I viewed it as being a good workplace community member.

One of the first questions that prospective employees ask is about benefits. I had health insurance for all of my real job work life. I define a real job as one with regular hours, like 9 to 5, and employees are paid regularly on the same day each month. The employer offers workers' benefits, including vacation days, sick leave, and health insurance. I had a designated lunch period and morning and afternoon "smoke" breaks. I didn't smoke, but used the 15 minutes to dial down.

I also became more aware of my uncertain financial future and applied for all kinds of part-time and full-time jobs. Even though I had 15 years of grant writing and administrative experience, the competition in a state of 3 million people was fierce.

*******

In 1995, I met Sally Martin, a Boulder City Council member, at a networking event. We talked about my consulting business. My first big contract was healthcare-related. She told me about the city council's plan to pass an ordinance banning indoor smoking. The Fresh Air Is A Right (FAIR) political action committee sought a campaign manager for the citywide vote. I didn't spend much time around cigarette smokers and was largely unaware of secondhand smoke, other than being annoyed by the rare instances I was around smokers.

She encouraged me to set up an office in her office suite. We shared services like a copy machine, the phone system, a receptionist, and a conference room. I got a slow start with FAIR. One day, I had to stay home with a high fever, puffy eyes, and a rash on my forehead.

"Go to the doctor," the receptionist ordered. I had an individual policy with KP and made an appointment.

"I'm not sure what that is," Dr. Lookner observed.

"Might it be shingles?" I asked.

"Probably not, you're only 42. You're not anywhere close to being old." The doctor told me to go home and rest. "Cold packs. Calamine lotion."

What he didn't know was that medicine hadn't quite pieced together that the chickenpox virus doesn't really go away. I think this was a mild case of shingles. After the chickenpox, the virus quietly had taken up residence in my nerves. I soon recovered and was ready to take on Big Tobacco.

In 1995, Boulder was at the crossroads of a fight that would pit public health against one of the most powerful industries in America. My contract with FAIR paid well, but not nearly as much as a regular job would have paid. The tasks included fundraising, marketing, and volunteer recruitment, which were my skills.

Sally suggested I legitimize myself and get an office with her at Walnut and Broadway. The suite occupied the entire floor of an office building, offering a copy machine, conference rooms, a kitchen, and a lobby area for dozens of sole proprietors. I acquired two Macintosh computers and decided to buy health insurance.

I remember my first days stepping into the campaign. The City Council had already passed the ordinance, but the ink was barely dry before the restaurant association and tobacco interests gathered enough signatures to force it onto the ballot. They thought they could crush the ordinance with scare tactics, warning of economic collapse, lost jobs, and shuttered businesses. Their budget dwarfed ours, but we had something they didn't: the truth, and a community ready for change.

Running FAIR's campaign was part strategy, part stamina, and part sheer grit. We knew we had to frame the issue not as one of rights taken away, but as rights expanded—the right of children to eat in restaurants without wheezing through a haze of smoke, the right of workers to make a living without inhaling carcinogens.

We were fueled by donated coffee and volunteer energy. Every night, we pored over voter rolls, planned neighborhood canvases, and trained volunteers to knock on doors. FAIR raised a few bucks, but our campaign wasn't glamorous and slick. Boulder responded. Families, teachers, doctors, and bartenders joined in, sharing their own stories of asthma attacks, scratchy throats, and long-term health fears.

The opposition's ads were slick and relentless. They painted FAIR as radicals trying to kill small businesses. But every time their message aired, we doubled down with testimony from local business owners who had already gone smoke-free and hadn't lost customers.

The opposition was at a disadvantage from the outset. According to the Centers for Disease Control (CDC), secondhand smoke causes nearly 34,000 premature deaths from heart disease yearly in the United States among adults who do not smoke. Nonsmokers exposed to secondhand smoke at home or on the job increased their risk of heart disease by 25 to 30 percent. Short doses of secondhand smoke damage blood vessel linings, which may lead to heart attacks. Besides, "Tobacco causes cancer ..." was printed on all tobacco products.

We held rallies, packed forums, and wrote letters to the *Daily Camera*. Our volunteers weren't just voters, but were neighbors telling neighbors why this mattered.

I etched that election night into my memory. The campaign had consumed us for months, and we'd braced ourselves for a nail-biter. But when the results came in, it wasn't close. FAIR had won handily. Boulder had spoken loud and clear: clean air mattered more than tobacco profits.

That victory was bigger than just one city ordinance. It was proof that grassroots campaigns could beat Big Tobacco, even when outspent. It put Boulder on the map as one of the first communities in the country to say no, decisively, to second-hand smoke. And for me, it was a turning point—an unforgettable reminder of the power of organized people, clear messaging, and the belief that health is a right, not a privilege.

FAIR's campaign wasn't only about smoke-free air. It was about a community finding its voice against an industry that had silenced too many for too long. And I'll always carry pride in knowing I helped orchestrate that winning effort.

*******

The successful FAIR campaign work evolved into a contract with an anti-tobacco use organization called Stay Healthy-Oppose Using Tobacco (SHOUT). The group issued SHOUT cards that were good for discounts at local businesses. The FDA made a deal with the tobacco companies.

Big tobacco quit advertising its products to kids in exchange for billions of dollars distributed to states. That put an end to many local efforts, as the states trickled down a few bucks to local efforts, but most remained under the control of the state to fund its bureaucracy.

The tobacco industry's marketing strategy continues to hook vulnerable adolescents. When I was growing up, tobacco companies advertised in comic books. There was always a bully who pushed around a kid with low self-esteem. They were encouraged to start smoking to be tougher and stronger. According to the FDA, among adult daily tobacco users, 90 percent began using tobacco by age 18. The FDA estimates that each day, 1,500 youth under 18 smoke their first cigarette.

Tobacco companies began consolidating and diversifying. In 1985, Philip Morris acquired General Foods in response to RJ Reynolds' merger with Nabisco. Three years later, Phillip Morris bought Kraft Foods. By the end of the decade, the FDA tobacco settlement was looming. Tobacco giants spun off their food divisions to avoid any liability from the tobacco industry's cover-up that smoking wasn't addictive.

Not only were there changes in the food industry, but significant changes were also occurring in healthcare during the 1990s. At that time, I didn't think anyone realized how a few large companies would eventually monopolize the healthcare industry.

When I quit working regular jobs and chose self-employment, I found health insurance to be a confusing topic. I was unaware of how to deal with doctors because when I had employer-provided insurance, I seldom used it.

Thanks to Sally Martin, my ECOS self-proprietorship started to grow. I had an office, a fax machine, and computers. It was time for me to get organized and sign up for a KP individual health insurance policy.

*******

In 1993, when I decided Boulder would be my new home, I made a mistake by transitioning from Wyoming to Colorado without giving it much thought. I was overconfident about my ability to find a job. I had a proven track record of raising money and writing grants, and was in good health at 40.

Being invincible, I believed it was okay that I didn't have steady insurance benefits. When I came back down to earth, I found it unsettling to wedge myself into the Colorado non-profit or public sector. If there was ever a time when I felt helpless, it was when my savings ran low, I had no health insurance, and I had no success finding work.

The rejection letters led me to entrepreneurship. I used my economic development skills to help pull myself up by my bootstraps. It was a "What have you done for me lately" world. I had to start from scratch.

ECOS combined my biology, political science, and multidisciplinary approach to problem-solving. That was my first stab at being a consultant. I took for granted workplace amenities like a computer, printer, copy machine, a phone, paid vacation, sick days, and health insurance.

The ECOS business plan aimed to manage cash flow by leveraging several contracts with overlapping completion dates. At first, I enjoyed waking up unemployed every morning and thinking about what I had to do to make money that day. I joined the "gig economy" before it became trendy.

My three regular jobs in Wyoming were stable even during transitions between stints because work found me.

# Chapter 21

# Arapaho Healing: Cedar Smoke and Chokecherries

My ECOS business had gained traction. I was now doing contract work with the Northern Arapaho Tribe, commuting to Lander and the Wind River Reservation in West Central Wyoming. I was working with a local group called the Next 500 Years (N5Y), established in 1993, marking the 500th anniversary of Columbus's landing near the islands off what is now the southeastern United States. I served as the liaison between the tribe and the Boulder community.

N5Y volunteers introduced me to a couple named David and Susan, who owned a company called Full Moon Fashion Accessories that sought Native American artwork to adorn a line of ponytail holders. I introduced them to several Northern Arapaho artisans who were able to quickly hand-bead the small medallions applied to leather strips that wrapped around long hair and secured with Velcro. Workers at the Full Moon factory in the San Luis Valley, in southwest Colorado, assembled the materials.

Full Moon hired me to work in the purchasing department, which included insurance through KP. That was good, but I was unsure about the business stability, so I kept my sole proprietorship KP policy. I was the company liaison with the Arapaho artisans. The job offered KP health insurance and a steady paycheck for a while. I was the liaison with the tribal artists. We were fulfilling the orders for beadwork, but soon it was evident that the business was struggling. Sensing that my time was short at Full Moon, I began thinking up other projects.

"Are you still working that farm with the Arapahos?" A former colleague named Mike called me at home in Lander. "There's a North American Free Trade Agreement (NAFTA) conference in Denver. I heard there will be business people there interested in making deals." President Clinton instigated NAFTA, which was agreed upon by Mexico and Canada.

I planned my next Boulder drive to coincide with the conference convened by U.S. Department of Commerce Secretary Ron Brown. The final session was a networking event featuring representatives from Mexican communities, who were seated at tables to discuss potential partnerships with their American counterparts.

When the conference concluded, most attendees departed. I sat down at a table with three fellows from Unión de Crédito Agropecuaria, Industrial y Comercial de Sombrerete (UCAICS), a credit union based in Sombrerete, Zacatecas, Mexico. We were able to communicate in a sort of Spanglish. We spoke about the high-grade alfalfa hay on the Arapaho Farm. The UCAICS guys were interested.

As the session ended, UCAICS invited me to Mexico. Traveling to Sombrerete was the first time I'd been to the interior. The only other time I'd been to Mexico was when a buddy and I drove from Laramie to San Diego for the 1987 Holiday Bowl football game between Wyoming and Iowa. We made a side trip to Tijuana for a night on the town.

Before my trip, I arranged for a ride to UCAICS from Durango, a city in the state of Durango, which is adjacent to Zacatecas. A travel agent arranged my visit. He booked a flight to Guadalajara rather than Durango or Zacatecas, both of which were two hours away from Sombrerete. I took a local Rojo de los Altos bus to Durango. That was the wrong choice. An express would have taken 10 hours instead of 13. I didn't know that the bus stopped in Sombrerete and could have saved a few more hours had I known to get off.

A UCAICS employee named Adolfo met me. He spoke good English. I practiced my Spanish with him. He was my guide and interpreter. Although UCAICS and I didn't accomplish much during my first visit, I established a relationship with the UCAICS manager, Faustino.

I became more familiar with the rural community, which was hungry for new job opportunities and less interested in improving their hay production. As it turned out, the weather is very arid and hot. Water came sporadically. Even dry land farming would be problematic.

*******

Upon my return to Boulder from Sombrerete, I talked with my Full Moon colleagues about what NAFTA could offer Full Moon in Mexico. David and Susan decided to close their manufacturing plant in southwest Colorado.

By this time, Full Moon was restructuring and had decided to close the ponytail holder factory in San Luis. My mission was to move the assembly operation to Sombrerete. I was spun off Full Moon as a contractor and resurrected ECOS, which "borrowed" the Full Moon equipment and set up the assembly in a building financed by UCAICS.

Over six years working half-time in Mexico, I had no significant medical issues. Healthcare availability was less accessible and less regulated. My mother worried about me living part-time in Mexico and kept reminding me that I didn't have health insurance that would be useful out of the U.S. She didn't want to get a call from the police department that they found me in a sleazy motel room with one less kidney.

I was contacted out of the blue by a small manufacturing company in Utah that made climbing wall handholds and was interested in making them in Sombrerete. The principal was a former Mormon Missionary in Mexico. His Spanish was good, and he felt at home in rural Zacatecas. He became very ill on one of our trips with a bad cold.

He and I went to the local *Farmacia*. He purchased a vial of penicillin and a syringe kit. The antibiotic was a thick fluid, and the needle and syringe reminded me of what my grandfather used to jab insulin into his thigh during the 1960s. My pal went into the dingy bathroom, and a few minutes later, he emerged with a limp. A few days later, he was back to health.

We discussed healthcare in Mexico. He explained that there are public clinics, but they can be a hassle for international visitors. Participation in the state insurance system was inexpensive but too expensive for many residents. There was quite a bit of self-care.

The sickest I became was from a bad *elote* I purchased from a Sombrerete street vendor. An *elote* is boiled corn on the cob dipped in Valentina hot sauce and coated with grated white cheese. They are very flavorful, including the one I ate that was bad, which resulted in stomach cramps, fever, and diarrhea. There was a closet-sized walk-up *Farmacia* that literally sold "over the counter." The *farmacéutico* handed me a yellow and white box of Bactrim. I took two of the large white tablets and immediately felt better, with no allergic reactions.

When I was on my 2013 deathbed and staving off infection, my medical record says I was allergic to Bactrim. Maybe the *Bactrim Hecho en Mexico* is different from other Bactrim.

After six years in business, my partner Faustino contracted stomach cancer. He and his family moved to Mexico City for better health care. He eventually died, and his brother, Francisco, took over the company and moved it in a different direction, ending my ties south of the border.

*******

ECOS and my Full Moon gig wouldn't have come about if it weren't for my last job in Wyoming with the Northern Arapaho Tribe, which evolved into my entrepreneurial pursuits in Colorado and Mexico. The tribe hired me to be its Community and Economic Development Director. By this time, I had established a strong track record of writing and securing grants from state and federal sources.

When I started with the tribe, I still lived in Lander, one of the Reservation's border towns. Wind River is a land mass larger than the state of Rhode Island that the Arapaho share with the Eastern Shoshone Tribe.

Working for the tribal government was more political than my previous two jobs. I attribute that to when the U.S. government forced tribes to live on reservations and learned Western governmental processes. I can't say I've bumped into a group of people more knowledgeable about parliamentary procedures.

I learned that the Arapaho have a direct relationship with the federal government, and funds flowed directly to the tribe, bypassing the state government. The grantwriting process was the same, but the players were different.

The Arapaho are a sovereign nation. Article 1, Section 8 of the United States Constitution says, "The Congress shall have the power to ... regulate commerce with foreign nations, and among the several states, and with the Indian tribes." The U.S. government has a direct relationship with tribes, including providing healthcare through the Indian Health Service (IHS).

The U.S. Congress created the IHS in the late 19th century to provide medical care to Native Americans. The IHS was initially part of the War Department and later became part of the Department of Health, Education, and Welfare (HEW). In 1955, HEW accepted the service during government reorganization. The IHS is now an agency within the Department of Health and Human Services' Public Health Service (PHS). The IHS provides acute medical care and has developed programs and initiatives to prevent and manage chronic conditions, such as diabetes and cardiovascular disease.

Just as I think everybody should work for a feminist group, my belief holds for spending time with the tribal government at some point in their life. That experience will open your eyes to the downside of Western expansion. While the Arapaho assimilated into the American Way of life at gunpoint, the tribe didn't forget its traditions and culture, which assimilation may have suppressed but did not exterminate.

A popularly elected Arapaho Business Council (ABC) handles much of the day-to-day business of the tribe. The tribe conducts an election every two years, and at times, there is a high turnover of council members. After one election, the ABC shifted its focus away from western-style job creation. It returned to relying on traditional ceremonies and the wisdom of spiritual elders to make decisions, leading to greater tribal prosperity. Restoring the tribal language and traditions was viewed as a form of community healing, completing the missing components of the tribal "cycle of life."

I was pretty well accepted into tribal affairs because I looked like an Arapaho, but wasn't related to anyone. The ABC eased me out of my role in economic development. It allowed me to continue as a consultant on the Arapaho Farm and the "Cultural Conduit." Tribes hired consultants for short-term expertise on various topics, including natural resources and social services.

I retained my Blue Cross - Blue Shield health insurance benefits, but I had to forgo vacation days, sick leave, and retirement contributions. On top of my health insurance, I could visit the IHS for over-the-counter drugs. The only time I stopped by was when I developed a bad cold and was provided a decongestant, now sold as Mucinex.

I was surprised to see IHS doctors and office staff wearing uniforms with bars and medals. The President commissions PHS Officer Corps members, who may wear uniforms similar to those of military personnel but with varying colors and different insignias. IHS doctors are typically Commanders or Captains.

The Cultural Conduit was consistent with the new tribal direction. A group of Arapaho artists, led by Eugene Ridgley Sr., created a body of work and other cultural offerings, including drummers, singers, and dancers. My part was to make arrangements with Boulder art galleries and craft stores to provide space where Arapaho artists could show and sell their work. Had the tribal elders not been involved, the project would never have happened.

*******

My experience was that the Arapaho are very communal. Friends and acquaintances often invited me to participate in sweat lodge purification and blessing ceremonies. I attended a sweat that wished goodwill for the Cultural Conduit's success, and the N5Y. It was ironic, because after the participants verbalized their good intentions, progress on the Cultural Conduit slowed down and soon came to a halt. Most likely, the project stalled due to some malicious intentions.

Ceremony participants request advice, healing, hope, and forgiveness, among other things. The lodge is dome-shaped and represents Mother Earth's womb. In the past, they were constructed from arced willow branches and covered with animal hides. Sweat leaders cover their modern lodges with skins, blankets, and tarps. The lodge's interior is sacredly prepared and groomed.

During the ceremony, the leader placed hot stones in the center pit and explained the purpose of the sweat while tossing cedar wood chips on the rocks. Aromatic cedar smoke filled the room and was very soothing. My practice was inhaling some and wafting smoke over my body.

The leader ladled sacred water over the stones before guiding the participants in prayer and song. Steam infused with the scent of cedar smoke soon filled the lodge. Depending on each participant's heat tolerance level, the lodge interior becomes steamy and hot. Since hot air rises, I flopped over and onto the floor to cool off. Like in a sauna, being aware of your well-being is essential.

Whenever I had the opportunity, I took sweat lodge hosts up on their offers to participate. Being among six or seven others expressing their specific and general concerns about life was very powerful. I doubt there's much research-based data about the effectiveness of being around all that powerful mental energy.

I've wondered about the medicinal benefits of cedar smoke. I've heard of research showing that medicinal smoke can eliminate bacteria on surfaces and those airborne with 90 percent effectiveness. Hospitals are one of the places with the highest levels of disease-causing crud and would benefit from cedar smoke.

A post-sweat Arapaho staple was fry bread dipped in chokecherry gravy. The chokecherry harvest was an annual summer event. The lush berry bushes grew along riverbanks and irrigation ditches. Tribal members traditionally combined the berries with dried meat to form pemmican. The Arapaho used chokecherries to treat respiratory ailments and to soothe sore throats. The juice is rich in antioxidants and possesses anti-diarrheal and astringent properties.

The N5Y sweat had not-so-positive results. The Cultural Conduit was successful until the group suddenly went out of business when the lead project consultant absconded with some of the group's assets and fled town.

*******

I knew from the first time I lived through this that my job with the Northern Arapaho would be a big balancing act. I should have thought twice about resigning from my position with the City of Lander government when there was a change in administrations. Regardless, I had decided that it was time for a change.

Another thing I learned is that when starting anew, I needed a safety net in place to catch me when I jumped off the entrepreneurial cliff. My work with Lander was fulfilling, especially facilitating an early merger in the healthcare industry, which required a challenging skill set that I developed on the job to complement my grant writing abilities.

# Chapter 22

# Healthcare Mergers: Sick Profits

Before joining the Northern Arapaho Tribe, my second job in the early 1980s was again in local government as Assistant to the Mayor of Lander, Wyoming. I was 27 and upwardly mobile. Moving to quiet and mellow Lander, nestled at the foot of the Wind River Range, was a big culture shock compared to Gillette, Wyoming, on the Northeast Wyoming plains, which moved at the speed of sound.

Legends of my grantwriting prowess preceded me. I was young, confident, healthy, and a little on the wild side, but surprisingly, I didn't hurt myself or others and rarely encountered the healthcare system. Some of my colleagues visit the doctor frequently.

"As long as I have health insurance, I might as well use it," was their attitude. I was the opposite and was seldom sick. The only time I had a headache was from too much El Presidente brandy and Coke during the pre-Christmas Posada holiday in Mexico.

While in Lander, my most critical health condition was the time I dislocated my shoulder from sliding into second base playing softball in a town league game. I played on a team comprised mostly of city employees called the Green Machine. We weren't that good, and I called us the Gangrene Maching. It didn't hurt, but it was strange having my arm dangling from my shoulder.

I drove to the Lander hospital, where the ER doctor placed me under mild anesthesia and popped it back into place. That was the first time I had taken the pain-killing drug Percocet. The doctor instructed me to be careful when driving home with my arm in a sling and to take the tablets as prescribed.

Driving home?

I don't remember much, except that I woke up the next day, and my shoulder hurt. I kept taking the prescribed medicine with no side effects, except that I felt dreamy and relaxed. A notice on the vial said, "May be habit forming." I didn't know what that meant since I hadn't used anything more potent than smoking weed. If I had a reason to self-medicate, I could get hooked on opiates.

That was the extent of my experience with the local medical community as a patient, but I became involved with the politics of healthcare. Some of the best specialty medical providers had based their practices in Lander.

*******

One of my job assignments was coordinating the city of Lander's economic development efforts. In 1979, the Three Mile Island nuclear power plant experienced a partial meltdown. That put a halt to Fremont County's uranium industry. There were also rumblings about the Atlantic City U.S. Steel taconite mine closing, which happened in 1983 when the labor force lost hundreds of mining jobs.

Top-quality health care was a community benefit touted in my economic diversification efforts. "Vigorous Retired" was a market of people who were no longer working but continued to lead vibrant lives and contribute to the economy with stable, fixed incomes.

In 1980 and 1981, turmoil arose among local doctors who were dissatisfied with the management of Bishop Randall Hospital by the nonprofit Lutheran Health and Home Society (LHHS).

At the time, I had no idea what might happen when healthcare became less of a public good and more about profit and stockholder dividends. The Fremont County experience was one of the early examples of hospitals evolving from public and nonprofit ownership into for-profit privatization.

There was a political rift since the Fremont County Hospital Board also managed the Riverton Memorial Hospital, also managed by LHHS, located 25 miles from Lander. I became involved in the issue when my boss, Mayor Del McOmie, appointed the Lander Hospital Commission to provide the city's perspective on the controversy.

The Fremont County hospital experiment foreshadowed the nationwide healthcare industrial complex managed care approach, which, theoretically, would reduce overhead costs by limiting patients to specific medical practitioners and hospitals. Hospital mergers increased from 12 in the 1980s to 24 per year in the 1990s.

Before mergers, insured patients selected care from a variety of independent providers. Insurance companies seldom questioned medical decisions. Most doctors were in solo practice or small groups. Physician and hospital fees-for-service were reimbursed based on average costs. The theory behind consolidation was that acquiring large patient groups and better-coordinated healthcare through mergers and acquisitions would reduce costs through economies of scale. Quality would improve from workflow efficiency.

There was a backlash from doctors who owned managed care plans with limited, flat-fee reimbursements, which lowered their profits. Medical service productivity declined after doctors evolved from entrepreneurs to employees.

It turned out that hospitals and management companies overpaid for properties and doctor practices. The management companies in the middle were supposed to add professionalism and efficiency, which turned out to be an overhead cost that cut into profits.

I'm not sure of the specific complaints from the Lander doctors, but the dispute reached the point where 20 physicians and a psychiatrist agreed to form a corporation and invest in a second Lander hospital in partnership with a for-profit company called Qualicare, based in New Orleans.

The Lander doctors' group would invest $19,000 into what would be called the Lander Valley Regional Medical Center (LVRMC), with the majority of the investment borne by Qualicare.

An initial board of directors consisting of three doctors, three Qualicare selections, and a community member would govern the venture. The medical representatives suggested were Steve Hauf, Hart Jacobson, and Mike Pryor. Dr. Pryor was my orthopedic surgeon who provided follow-up care for my dislocated shoulder.

According to newspaper accounts, despite the word on the street that the local medical community was dissatisfied with LHHS, Dr. Jacobson insisted that the project would provide more beds in Lander.

Riverton Memorial Hospital was also involved in the controversy. Lander and Riverton have been community rivals for generations. The LVRMC group believed that a new hospital would be preferable to a countywide ballot issue to expand Bishop Randall Hospital by raising bond funds, which Riverton voters would likely oppose unless the County Commissioners allocated some of the bond funds to Riverton Memorial.

The Fremont County Hospital Board ousted LHHS and placed a moratorium on capital expansion. Later in 1981, the Lander Hospital Commission agreed with the eventual outcome. The final board of directors consisted of two doctors, the medical chief of staff, two representatives from Qualicare, and a resident from the Lander Hospital Commission. Bishop Randall Hospital was closed in favor of the new LVRMC hospital development by Qualicare and the local doctors' group.

Government grants were a traditional economic development tool used to entice new businesses to relocate or existing ones to expand. The city provided the LVRMC with the hospital site on a piece of public airport land. My job was to secure funding by leveraging grants for public services, such as waterlines and the construction of Bishop Randall Drive, with private sector funding.

Chapter 23

# Accidental EMT: A Crash and CPR

Before my stints with the Northern Arapaho Tribe and the City of Lander, my first job was as a member of the Wyoming Human Services Project (WHSP) team in Gillette, Wyoming. We worked half-time with a local agency, in my case as an Assistant to the City Administrator.

Although I was a political science major, I didn't know much about local government. My last class in grad school was Public Administration 101.

That didn't help me with my assigned task to write grants. I didn't know anything about that either when Joe, the Planning Director, handed me a section for the Federal Register for a grant from the Farmers' Home Administration in the U.S. Department of Agriculture. I followed the instructions and had my first grant funded. I think it was $14,000.

That was a confidence builder.

The remaining time I spent with my WHSP team. We applied our diverse experiences and multidisciplinary perspectives to address local service gaps. These efforts included providing social work assistance, coordinating health services, and developing public recreation programs.

It was a rite of passage because this was the first time I felt emancipated from my parents. I no longer had to rely on them to pay for my medical care. Social interactions may increase longevity and improve brain health, but the outcomes differed among 25-year-old men with too much money and nowhere to spend it. Intentional socializing was the norm in Gillette because housing was expensive and in short supply.

One of my WHSP group members was a newly appointed attorney named Phil. His buddy Tom, also an attorney, was a Vietnam veteran who followed him to Gillette. We crammed into a rental house when we first came to town. Tom became claustrophobic, living on top of a group of guys. He had G.I. Bill benefits and suggested that he, Phil, and I chip in and purchase a house together.

Our home became known as the "3003 Club: Where Mom Is Never Home." Our interactions focused more on the social part and less on longevity and improved brain health. Based on my risky behavior, even though I had health insurance, I didn't think about taking care of myself.

*******

The most severe car accident I'd experienced was in Gillette. While standing at a stoplight, an oil field truck slammed into my sky blue Ford Pinto station wagon. The accident occurred after work. The streets were busy with shift changes, coal mine and oil field traffic rolling through town in big rigs, service trucks, and water haulers. My little Pinto sat so low to the ground that it felt like I was driving half-hidden beneath the shadow of taller vehicles.

I had pulled up to the intersection near Ole's Pizza, waiting for the light to change. A huge oilfield water truck barreled up behind me. Whether the driver was tired from a long day in the patch, distracted, or didn't see me in that squat little Pinto, I'll never know.

All I felt was the violent jolt of his bumper slamming into my rear end, the sudden snap of my head forward and back, and the fear that my car might crumple like a soda can under the weight of all that steel and water, or worse, explode. Pintos were known to ignite when the differential bolts punctured the plastic gas tank.

Miraculously, it didn't. I got out, shaky but standing, and looked at the damage. The Pinto's bumper was bent, the right rear quarter panel had a crease, and the truck was barely scratched. The driver climbed down from his cab, apologetic, and we exchanged insurance information. We didn't call the cops, but should have. An ambulance would have responded. Instead, I checked myself over. I had no broken bones, no blood, no immediate pain. I drove away thinking how lucky I was to be alive, let alone unhurt.

With rear-end collisions, luck isn't always obvious right away. Whiplash can be one of those injuries that sneak up on you. You don't always feel it until days later, when the muscles seize or the spine begins to ache. Many people who walk away from wrecks like mine end up carrying headaches, stiffness, or even arthritis for the rest of their lives.

That day, I escaped all of it. No lingering pain, no lasting injury. Just the memory of how close I'd come to being crushed by a truck that probably weighed twenty times more than my Pinto.

I realized how fragile that line is between fortune and misfortune. In Gillette that evening. Had my car caught on fire, I would have been happy to have health insurance.

As it was, the trucking company was reluctant to pay, and my housemate Tom sent a lawyerly letter. I soon received a check in the mail. I walked away from that ordeal unscathed, which contributed to my youthful hubris.

******

My city government colleague, Richard, was the personnel officer. He was responsible for negotiating our group health insurance plan. Richard also set up in-service workshops, including basic First Aid and CPR training. The Gillette firefighter who presented the class stated that there was a shortage of Emergency Medical Technicians (EMTs) because many community-based EMTs had quit, opting for higher-paying jobs at the coal mines.

I took this information to the WHSP team as a gap in community service. After discussing it with my colleagues, I decided to enroll in the EMT training class. I had a long-standing interest in medicine, having been the student manager for my high school wrestling team. After graduating from high school, I originally planned to complete a pre-med curriculum in college. I didn't last long in that highly competitive major, but I always wanted to be involved in the medical field, and I enrolled in the county EMT training class.

After I completed the coursework, the program required each student to ride along for a shift on a Campbell County Memorial Hospital ambulance. Since I had a day job, my tour was the eight-hour night shift. It was a weekday and uneventful. We drove around, but mostly parked and talked.

When we returned to the Emergency Medical Services garage, the shift supervisor handed me my EMT-I patch and certificate that I still have, dated April 12, 1980. He said the County would hire me on the spot, but I declined, knowing that this would be a fallback should I need to find work.

*******

One day, I was at Decker's grocery store and rolling my cart down a deserted aisle when I encountered a thin woman wearing a grayish plaid shirt and blue jeans on the linoleum floor. She had stopped breathing, her eyes were frozen open, and her face and hands were blue. I didn't know how long she had been unconscious.

In my EMT class, we practiced Cardio-Pulmonary Resuscitation (CPR) on a life-size doll named Rescuci-Annie, manufactured by Laerdal. There was also Rescuci-Andy and a youth version called Rescuci-Junior. The vintage full-body manikins had arms and legs clad in a blue jumpsuit. The new versions are the trunk and head.

I cleared her mouth with my index finger, then tilted her head back. She exhaled a puff of air when her airway was open, just as my instructor had mentioned. She was breathing, so I didn't have to apply chest compressions. I stayed with her, kept talking, holding steady until the sirens screamed closer and the EMTs arrived.

It wasn't heroism. It was a matter of remembering what to do. Without that EMT class, I might have stood there and waited.

That moment drove home what the statistics have been saying all along. In the U.S., more than 350,000 people collapse from sudden cardiac arrest outside hospitals every year. Most don't survive, but survival rates more than double when bystanders act. People who receive bystander CPR are almost four times more likely to live. Yet fewer than half of victims get help before the professionals arrive.

The gaps are glaring. Women are less likely to receive CPR from strangers. Black and Hispanic Americans are less likely to be helped, especially at home. Geography plays a role too—your chances of surviving can depend on whether you happen to collapse in a city that invests in public training or in a small town where fewer people know what to do.

It's a strange contrast. On one hand, something as simple as opening an airway or pressing down on a chest can mean the difference between life and death. On the other hand, the healthcare system itself has evolved into a sprawling, expensive, and inaccessible labyrinth, often indifferent to the very people it claims to serve. In that grocery store aisle, the system didn't matter. Insurance cards, hospital mergers, Medicaid expansions—none of it was relevant in the seconds that counted. All that mattered was a pair of hands and a little bit of training.

That day taught me something I carried with me: healthcare isn't just about the professionals in scrubs or the billion-dollar institutions. Sometimes it's about ordinary people stepping across the invisible line from bystander to participant. Sometimes it's about refusing to wait for permission to do good.

She was still unconscious, and I waited with her for a moment. I imagined that someone had called the police. There was no 911 back then. The EMTs soon wheeled a gurney around the corner and had the situation under control. I mentioned that I opened her airway and returned to my shopping. I have often wondered who my patient in Gillette was and if she paid the favor forward.

Thinking back, I took a similar First Aid class in grad school. I was an actor in the campus disaster simulation. My role was a guy who survived a car crash with a sucking chest wound. I strapped a piece of molded rubber in the form of a gaping bloody gash with a tube that oozed foamy red fluid filtered through a sponge.

The real-world CPR rescue in Gillette was my first memorable experience with the healthcare system from the other side of the stretcher. I had imagined being in the medical profession in college.

# Chapter 24

# College Daze: Healthcare Debate

How did I end up in Gillette? I sat out the post-Vietnam War recession in graduate school at the University of Wyoming. My mission while at the UW for two years was to take as many classes that offered internship experience. One day, I was walking through the student union and came across a table with a sign that read something to the effect of "Do you want a job after graduation? Join the Wyoming Human Services Project team."

That sounded like the way to go for me. I took two semesters of classes that focused on a multidisciplinary approach to decision-making. I had no idea what to expect. My team members learned how to work together and solve problems in small communities affected by rapid population growth due to the booming coal mining industry.

I applied at the last minute to the Department of Political Science.

Even though my GRE scores were terrible, the Political Science Department accepted me, but there were no grants or scholarships available. Then, shortly before classes began, the registrar informed me that a teaching assistantship had become available. That meant UW covered my tuition, and I would receive a teaching stipend. I happily accepted.

My parents let me live with them for what turned out to be two years. They were happy to have me around and hoped my advanced degree would improve my job prospects. Around this time, the concept of primary healthcare was emerging.

My mom had a job on campus in the College of Commerce and Industry that offered excellent insurance benefits. My dad had a minimal policy provided by Coca-Cola, with the gap covered under Mom's policy. Since my sister and I weren't legally emancipated, Mom's insurance plan covered us. I could also use the campus infirmary, which I never visited. I also didn't have a doctor in Laramie.

*******

After graduating from Hastings College in Hastings, Nebraska, I didn't know what I wanted to do with my life. There were no employment opportunities in my fields of study. The most practical thing I did as a biology major was to count smooth and wrinkled peas. Nor was there work discussing the benefits of the confederation form of government that I gleaned from the political science department.

I thought about taking the Civil Service test. Maybe I'd like to be a spy for the CIA or sort mail at the U.S. Postal Service. I took the Graduate Record Exam (GRE), believing that the UW graduate school was my best option.

I spent four years at Hastings College without any medical issues and didn't have a doctor. Health insurance wasn't on my radar screen. There was a medical clinic on campus that I never visited, mainly because I didn't know where it was.

Hastings was a disciplined and socially conservative school. Risky behavior wasn't a community norm at Hastings. For example, school rules required women to return to the dorms by a particular hour. Even the rowdiest times were sedate. My fraternity, Eta Phi Lambda, had pledge training for the incoming members and an initiation ceremony. Both were humorously humiliating but not violent, nor was there much excessive drinking involved.

I had given up sports, but I missed the competition, so I joined the Hastings College speech team. Preparing for weekly debate tournaments was highly competitive, but no sweating from being in a hot wrestling room.

Nor did I get sick or admit to being sick during my college years. If I were, I wouldn't have told anyone because I didn't want to lose my spot on the team. Like in athletics, someone was rehearsing on the sidelines and ready to step up.

When I was a sophomore, the national debate resolution that year was: RESOLVED: That the federal government should provide a comprehensive medical care program for all its citizens. It wasn't just an academic exercise. The same question was being argued in Washington, D.C. Senator Ted Kennedy had just published *In Critical Condition,* a blistering critique of American medicine. Kennedy made no bones about the morally wrong, fractured, and inequitable nature of the healthcare system. He argued that healthcare should be a right, not a privilege.

For my affirmative debate case, I leaned on what felt like the most promising idea on the horizon: the Health Maintenance Organization (HMO). Kaiser Permanente in California was the standout example. Its prepaid, preventive-care model is a way to provide comprehensive coverage while keeping costs in check. To me, it looked like the logical path toward fulfilling Kennedy's vision.

The negative debaters were ruthless. They portrayed HMOs as impersonal machines where patients waited in endless lines, saw whichever doctor happened to be on duty, and were treated more like numbers than people.

They went further, holding up European health systems as cautionary tales of bloated budgets and inefficient services. Against that backdrop, they claimed American private insurers were the pinnacle of efficiency and innovation.

At the time, I didn't have the hindsight to see how selective that argument was, but it sharpened my understanding that debates were as much about values and perceptions as they were about facts.

Meanwhile, in the real world, President Richard Nixon had proposed a sweeping health reform plan that, on paper, wasn't far from Kennedy's ideas. Nixon's strategy relied on the private sector but required employers to provide insurance to their workers, with the federal government stepping in to cover those who were left out. It was a public–private partnership, blending mandates with subsidies.

Nixon proposed that all employers would be required to participate in a national Assisted Health Insurance program. The measure would have replaced Medicaid and included financial subsidies to people who couldn't afford insurance. The plan capped out-of-pocket expenses and eliminated exclusions for pre-existing conditions.

Kennedy, by contrast, favored a publicly funded single-payer system, closer to what Europe and Canada were doing at the time.

For a brief moment, there was daylight for compromise. Kennedy later admitted that Nixon's plan was probably the closest America ever came to enacting universal healthcare, but the timing wasn't in sync. Nixon was drowning in the Watergate conspiracy that resulted in his resignation as President on August 9, 1974.

The drowning of Mary Jo Kopechne on July 18, 1969, was Kennedy's dire straits. The two were driving on Chappaquiddick Island when his Oldsmobile careened off the Dike Bridge and into the Poucha Pond. Kennedy survived and swam to safety, but Kopechne drowned. Kennedy did not report the incident to the police until the following morning. He was charged with leaving the scene of an accident causing personal injury, and pleaded guilty. The court suspended a two-month jail sentence.

Neither man had the political capital to carry the reform across the finish line. The grand bargain collapsed under the weight of its flaws.

Looking back, I find it ironic. While I was at Hastings arguing about HMOs versus private insurance, the country came within a hair's breadth of systemic reform. Nixon's proposal could have been the foundation of an American universal health system, but scandal and mistrust pushed it off the table. In its place, the same patchwork system Kennedy called "in critical condition" limped forward, leaving later generations, including my own, to wrestle with the same questions.

*******

Other than researching the debate topic, that would be the only contact I'd have with the expanding health care industrial complex. One Winter Break, my grandparents invited my family over for Christmas. The usual gift I gave to Grandpa Sakata was a bottle of Aqua Velva aftershave lotion and a can of Colgate amalgamated toothpaste. He gave me a wrapped-up container of some stuff I didn't know about. After we opened gifts before breakfast, he drew a glass of water from the tap and added a spoonful of tannish powder from the container.

"What's this?" I asked.

"It's Metamucil. It keeps me regular. Good for the digestion." I gave it a try, and much to my surprise, I learned the next morning that what he said was true. I was hooked.

I adopted my grandfather's healthy colon scrubber, which was one of the only practical things I learned in college. Life is unknown and circuitous. I wouldn't have guessed in a million years what would happen after I turned 18, and my parents kicked me out of the nest and expected me to figure the future out for myself.

I had no idea what I was going to do 600 miles from home in the middle of Nebraska. I did become an ardent Nebraska Cornhusker football fan.

Most of my friends had a pretty good idea what they wanted to do with their lives. I wasn't paying attention. My future was a blank page.

GO BIG RED!

# Chapter 25

# School Daze: Bumps and Bruises

I was aging and was finally young enough to graduate from Cheyenne East High School. My interests were writing. I wrote for the *Thunderbolt* newspaper and also served as its cartoonist. I was a naturally good artist, too. There wasn't much money in either of those professions.

The only time I talked to a high school guidance counselor was when the basketball coach summoned me into his office. He informed me that I had enough credits to graduate.

As a late bloomer, during my junior and senior years, I overloaded my course load with numerous science classes, with my sights set on studying pre-med because my newly found science classmates talked about their ambitions to become medical doctors.

I decided to enroll at Hastings College, a Presbyterian-affiliated institution in Nebraska. Some of my buddies from the First Presbyterian Church, including Randy Johnston, the son of my ophthalmologist. He eventually wanted to take over his dad's practice. My friend Tad, whose father was also an MD, started at Hastings in pre-med.

*******

I did get a taste of the medical profession in high school. Wrestling was my fall and winter activity at East. I had no intention of participating in competitive collegiate athletics. One of my coaches took me on a recruiting trip to Colorado State University. I was an okay wrestler, but not a great one. I could have made the squad, but would have spent most of my college career on the "scout" team and been tossed around the mat by the stud wrestler from Iowa in my weight class.

As a senior, I was the heir apparent to the varsity team in the 112-pound weight class. The Laramie County School District # altered the school boundary in 1971 when federal busing legislation mandated school integration. The reconfiguration sent students from Johnson Junior High on the Southside who would have attended Central High to East. One of the transfers was an outstanding wrestler named Casey, who was in my natural weight class. We wrestled a few times, and he was better and stronger than I was.

My alternative was to lose five pounds and qualify for the 107-pound weight class. I was a skinny guy, and dropping that much weight would be a challenge. I was on a no-carbohydrate diet during the season.

The last time I saw Dr. Cohen was when I needed a prescription for a diuretic so I could piss out water weight. When I graduated from high school, Dr. Cohen was leaving private practice. Governor Stan Hathaway had appointed him to lead the Wyoming Department of Health.

I had a speech prepared explaining that this was temporary and the weight class poundage limit would increase in a few months. When I handed the doctor the red card, he signed it without reading it and sent me on my way. My first and only experience with athletic corruption.

As it turned out, Casey won the first of three state championships that year. I took third at 107. The life skill I learned from competitive wrestling was how to drop pounds quickly by cutting out carbohydrates to maintain weight.

In my junior year, I was back to full strength coming off an injury. I checked my leg length. One was still slightly longer than the other. My muscles were stronger, but I knew that re-injuring my back was still a possibility. I decided to stay at the Junior Varsity (JV) level, knowing that getting injured would be a low probability.

*******

The year before, as a sophomore, I twisted my spine during one practice while performing the Guillotine move. My lower back ached, and I could barely move, so I spent the rest of that after-school practice on my back. The spasms finally went away. I was able to shower, but drying off was a different story. Drying off was painful, and I rode my bike home sopping wet. My dad had a similar lower back issue and took me for the first time to his chiropractor, Dr. Woods.

When I went to his office, that visit was my first visit to a doctor other than my pediatrician, Dr. Cohen. I didn't know what to expect. When it was my turn, the nurse entered the waiting area and escorted me to the treatment room for some X-rays. She sat me down on a green leather upholstered table. Dr. Woods was a thin fellow with wire-framed glasses and slicked-back hair. His white jacket reminded me of the one my barber, Rube, used to wear.

"Maybe he's going to let my blood," I thought about the trivial tidbit I learned during Medieval times, barbers were allowed to drain blood from people with various disorders. Barber poles are red and blue striped to signify veins and arteries. He entered the room with an envelope containing my X-rays and clipped them on the illuminator.

"You have a slightly curved spine," he said, pointing to the image of my lumbar vertebrae before pulling my legs toward him. "See here? Because of it, your right leg is half an inch longer than the other." The doctor asked me to lie face down on his flexion treatment table, placing two electrodes on my lower back that sent electrical pulses to my tight muscles. He soon returned and proceeded to crack my bones. The noise was startling, but the releases felt good across my shoulders, down my spine to my pelvis.

Dr. Woods lined up my legs when he finished torturing me. They were back to being the same length, and the pain was gone. I had one or two more treatments and then a follow-up evaluation.

"I don't think you should wrestle anymore this season," Dr. Woods commanded. "Your back may slip out again unless you're careful. I suggest you walk between treatments. Walking between classes and around the school would suffice. If you're a wrestler, you know about gentle back bridges and leg lifts. Do a few of those every day. It'll hurt when you start, so be slow about it."

Dr. Woods allowed me to attend practice and work out at half-speed. Coach Phillips asked if I wanted to be the student manager.

"What's that about?" I asked. The coach explained that I would be responsible for maintaining and restocking the medical kit before each match. "If one of the guys gets injured, you'll help me with any treatment. You'll also keep track of each match and write down the scores in the book."

I jumped at the opportunity. There weren't many sophomores who made the Varsity or JV team. I still wore braces, which was a problem because I was conscious about them and had to be careful when an opponent cross-faced me and risk cutting my inner mouth on the steel bands.

The main benefit of being the student trainer was making the road trips, which meant staying in motels and dining on

delicacies like hot beef sandwiches. Although it wasn't required, I took an introductory First Aid class offered at my
church.

Midway through the season, I wondered what we would do
if a kid broke an ankle, fainted on the mat, or experienced a
medical issue beyond what I could provide from my wooden kit
covered with a fake black leather veneer. I was up for that challenge.

"What if a fan in the bleachers had a heart attack or fell
down the steps?" I wondered. Whether home or away, I made it
a point to find the pay phones and, if there was a phone in the
coach's office.

During my sophomore year, when I served as team trainer,
bloody noses were the only on-the-mat injuries that required
my assistance. There was plenty of cotton in the medical kit to
stop the bleeding. Back then, bloodborne pathogens weren't a
concern, so rubber surgical gloves were not required. Sometimes one of the guys had a tight muscle, and I rubbed on an
analgesic ointment called Atomic Balm. I learned how to tape
ankles and fingers.

Chapter 26

# Dental Drills: Experimental Extraction

Another sign of my youthful un-aging was my poor dental health. My orthodontist, Dr. Gorny, finally removed my braces when I was a sophomore after the wrestling season. Three years of agonizing dental pain later, my teeth were much straighter than before. I had to wear retainers to keep my teeth from reverting to their original crooked position, which was a huge relief.

It's always something. A dental X-ray showed that the wisdom teeth buried in the left side of my mouth had grown and crowded my back molars.

The generally accepted procedure at the time was to remove the molar and the wisdom tooth. Rather than extract both teeth, Dr. Carson read an academic article about a method that would save one of them. He enlisted assistance from another dentist in town, Dr. Accardo, who lived up the block from us on Cactus Hill Road.

I imagine Dr. Carson explained the surgical plan to my parents, but I didn't know what was about to happen. By this time in life, needles didn't freak me out. The doctor jabbed me with a needle and deadened the left side of my head. Dr. Carson used a jagged drill to cut my molar in half. I couldn't feel the pain but felt the strange drilling sensation resonate through my skull.

Dr. Accardo steadied my head as Dr. Carson pulled out a stainless steel chisel and a mallet. He hammered away at the healthy molar. I couldn't feel that either, but I sensed my head bouncing around the neck cradle at the back of the chair. The hammering disintegrated the tooth and picked the pieces out with a pair of stainless steel pliers.

The objective of the surgery was to fill the gap created by the emerging wisdom tooth. Dr. Carson repositioned the tooth by prying it into the space where the molar had once been rooted. I could sense that I was bleeding profusely. That was that. I was in pain for two weeks, which I alleviated with aspirin.

Orthodontists at the time were unaware of the problems posed by tooth extraction. Dr. Gorny admitted later that before applying my braces, the X-rays had shown the Wisdom Teeth, but he assumed they would remain dormant, like the tooth in the roof of my mouth. He graciously offered a "redo." My parents would have preferred a refund. Not only was I not interested in another three years of pain, but I was going away to college, and scheduling periodic appointments posed a logistical problem.

*******

My parents had chosen Dr. Carson because he was a pediatric dentist. His office was a few doors up from Dr. Cohen's. My dad had terrible teeth, and I took after him. That meant I went to the dentist every couple of months. Dr. Carson was pleasant and not too scary.

The face of the office, though, was the dental hygienist and my aunt Elsie. Her calm demeanor was the primary reason that much of the office's business focused on pediatrics. I attribute that to the skills gained from managing our large extended family.

Her parents — my grandparents — emigrated from Japan. The Wyoming Alien Land Act was signed into law in 1946, shortly after the end of World War II, and prohibited aliens from purchasing real estate.

Elsie was native-born in Monte Vista, Colorado, and, on behalf of her parents, bought their home in south Cheyenne, where she lived with them and her brother, Richard. There were aunts, uncles, and their friends, my sister, me, and our five local cousins who frequented the family headquarters. In the summer, that number rose to a dozen or more. Elsie had referred my relatives to Dr. Carson.

Teeth cleaning was the first step during any dental appointment. Elsie placed an upholstered board across the chair arms. The child seat was the same type my barber, Rube, used when I would get haircuts. Dentistry was barbaric when I was young. The stainless steel probes and the little mirrors hadn't changed much over the centuries. The drills were belt-driven, and a foot pedal controlled the rotational speed of the bit.

A hose squirted water through a tiny nozzle. Elsie's trick was to see if she could hit my mouth from at least three feet away. It was like the carnival squirt gun game, shooting water into a clown's mouth to inflate a balloon. After swishing, the water was spit into a round ceramic cuspidor.

Water spewed from a stainless steel tube and swirled around the tiny sink, creating a fine aerosol mist. She poked around my teeth and scraped off the crud from under my gums before polishing them with a rubber applicator covered with a dab of gritty toothpaste attached to the variable-speed brace.

When Elsie finished, Dr. Carson took his turn with the probe. If I had X-rays taken, he would review them on the small illuminator. I generally had at least one cavity. Sometimes I had time to have it filled, but most of the time, I would have to return.

Dr. Carson's amiable disposition wasn't enough to put me at ease. The doctor sometimes dispatched Auntie Elsie to distract me when the anesthetic needle was inserted into my mouth before the drilling began. It got to the point that fillings weren't good enough, and my "baby teeth" deteriorated to the point that I had them covered with stainless steel caps. He did his best to keep my permanent teeth from growing too crooked.

I was walking proof that James Nestor's idea about how prepared food caused weak jaws, smaller mouths, and crooked teeth was accurate. There was nothing the doctor could do about my small mouth. Had I been breastfed and weaned on regular food, my mouth would likely have grown larger, and my jaw muscles would have been stronger.

*******

As I aged into Carey Junior High School as a 7th grader, my permanent teeth had grown too large for my head. Growing lower molars in the back of my mouth crowded the other teeth. Dr. Carson didn't consult with me about it, but I'm sure he advised my parents that I was a candidate for braces. He referred me to a traditional orthodontist, Dr. Gorny. My mom drove me to the Hynds Building in Downtown Cheyenne, located at the corner of Capitol Avenue and West 16th Street, for my initial consultation.

Dentists didn't scare me, considering the wretched condition of my teeth. I could handle any poking, prodding, and jabbing any dental sadist had to offer. I didn't know what to expect when I went for my first appointment. Dr. Gorny provided an overview of his process, which began with a 360-degree X-ray revealing that I had tiny Wisdom Teeth and an outlying tooth embedded above the roof of my mouth.

Next, he made plaster casts of my dentition. I returned later to see those. The casts indicated insufficient space for my teeth to migrate into. The objective was to improve my "bite" by straightening my teeth. In so doing, he had Dr. Carson pull out one of my lower incisors.

Rather than extraction, Nestor says that, as a child, it would have been better if my dentist had expanded my palate to make room. Removing the tooth not only delayed my braces for a few weeks but also didn't do anything to enlarge my mouth, which would ultimately become a problem. Dr. Gorny cemented tooth brackets onto the face of each tooth and wrapped steel bands around my molars to anchor the thicker arch wire threaded through the brackets. Thin stainless steel wires that secured each arch-wire into place when tightened by a small pair of pliers.

The first time I came home with my braces in place, our dinner was fried chicken. The first bite I took sent shock waves through my head. I couldn't eat anything solid for a few days until the teeth had positioned themselves. As my teeth subtly shifted, I returned to replace the tightening wires. Each tightening cost $25, which I delivered in a small yellow envelope.

The bracket wires interfered with my lifestyle by irritating my lips, and during wrestling season, I had to cover the braces with thin strips of wax provided by Dr. Gorny.

Now that I was in the twilight of my life in a teenager's body, it didn't matter that my teeth were crooked and my eyesight had much to be desired. My folks spent time and money on braces and glasses, but avoided telling me anything about the birds and bees.

Chapter 27

# Sex Lessons in Silence: Birds, Bees, and Betty

It wasn't until I was at Carey Junior High School that my classmates and I were required to take a class about sex education. The Physical Education teachers taught the health classes. I imagine that was because the school segregated the classes by gender. I don't recall any controversies about that. My parents would rather I learned about such things from experts, like the Driver's Education teacher, who was also the track coach.

Sex education in America has always been a battleground of culture, politics, and generational anxiety.

In the early 20th century, what schools called "sex hygiene" mainly was about disease prevention. During World War I, the Army taught soldiers about syphilis and gonorrhea. By the 1920s and 1930s, public health officials and reformers advocated for more comprehensive education about human reproduction. Many communities preferred to leave that "talk" to parents, clergy, or to no one at all.

Organizations such as the American Social Hygiene Association and Planned Parenthood began providing educational materials for schools in the 1940s and 1950s. These lessons were still primarily focused on anatomy and morality, rather than engaging in open discussions about relationships or sexuality.

Sex education expanded in Cheyenne when I was in junior high school. The Baby Boom had filled classrooms, teen pregnancy rates were climbing, and the sexual revolution was stirring. In 1964, the U.S. Office of Education endorsed sex education programs, and the number of schools offering them began to rise. The School District required a basic curriculum that emphasized biology.

*******

My teacher was Mr. Sam Contos, a neighbor of mine. He and his family lived on the corner of Windmill and Old Trail roads in the Cole Addition of Cheyenne. Sam and his wife, Stella, had a son and a daughter, who were much younger than I. Mr. Contos put in a good word with the manager of the Hitching Post Inn, who hired me for my first job as a busboy.

Sam was a cheerful and friendly guy, but he wore his game face at school. I hadn't seen him behave more seriously than when he was teaching my sex education class. He showed no preference for any of the neighborhood kids. In one class, I recall viewing a graphic black and white 16 mm movie about intimate body parts, sperm, and egg fertilization.

One of the most memorable and uneasy lessons was about masturbation. By then, most of the boys had already figured it out, though no one admitted it out loud.

"You shouldn't do it. You shouldn't pleasure yourselves." When Mr. Contos raised the subject, his tone was stern and commanding. He offered no explanation beyond vague warnings about self-control, morality, and wasting our energy.

What struck me wasn't the message, but the silence that wrapped around it. The unspoken norm was that desire itself was something to be feared, hidden, or disciplined. Pleasure

was treated as shameful, something that belonged in the shad-
ows. In a classroom full of restless boys, the subtext was clear:
don't talk about it, don't admit it, and certainly don't imagine it
could be normal.

The lessons weren't about biology, but were about control. It
was another way the culture of the time drew boundaries
around what was acceptable and what wasn't. Because no one
dared to question it, we carried those silences with us, tucked
into the corners of our private lives.

"Do not self-pleasure yourself," Mr. Contos commanded after the film screened, which discussed wet dreams and related
topics. I don't think he gave any reasons. By this time, I'd figured out masturbation and didn't understand what was so
wrong with that. My first experience was jerking off while fan-
tasizing about Betty Cooper, the blonde girl from *Archie* comic
books. All the guys snickered and looked around at each other.
It's not as if self-pleasure was a complete unknown.

I don't know what happened in the girls' version of the
class, but this is supposedly an excerpt from a 1960s sex education textbook.

"When he reaches his moment of fulfillment, a small moan
from yourself is encouraging to him and quite sufficient to indicate any enjoyment that you may have had," is one of the
tips suggested. "But remember to look your best when going to
bed. Try to achieve a look that is welcoming without being obvious. If you need to apply face cream or hair rollers, wait until
he is asleep, as this can be shocking to a man, the last thing at
night."

When the family went to bed, my parents had the door
closed. Closed bedroom doors must have been a house rule.
One of my friends walked in on his parents going at it. They
were mutually surprised. He said his parents were saying "good
night" to each other. That was a pretty good line. I always

closed my door, too, so I could read my comic books in the privacy of my room.

Mr. Contos taught us about reproduction and "the birds and the bees," but there was nothing about pleasure, consent, or contraception. The focus was on avoiding trouble from pregnancy, disease, or social shame.

The lessons ended with the assumption that someday we'd all grow up, get married, and have families. That was the path, laid out as clearly as the diagrams in our textbooks. But for me, that future was easier said than done.

*******

At the time, marriages between Asians and Caucasians were against the law in Wyoming. The State Legislature repealed the ban in 1964, but the weight of history lingered. Even when the law changed, attitudes didn't change overnight. The Supreme Court's landmark decision in *Loving v. Virginia* struck down laws prohibiting interracial marriage as unconstitutional in 1967. Until then, who you were allowed to love was dictated not by the heart, but by the law.

When my classmates were awkwardly joking about dating, I wasn't. The unspoken truth was that those options weren't really open to me. I realized how much of that silence shaped me. Sex education was never just about anatomy or reproduction. It was also about who counted, who belonged, and what kind of life was possible. As an adolescent, my parents didn't explain anything about interpersonal relationships. That was a sign of the times. Interracial relationships were new. Society hadn't yet caught up with new laws.

In my sex education classes, the subject matter was narrowed down to biology, reproduction, and a vague warning about what could go wrong if you weren't careful. What was most striking, looking back, was what wasn't there.

Not only were interracial relationships taboo, but Mr. Contos never discussed gender identity. I had no idea that there might be a continuum between male and female, or that attraction itself could take many forms, which the curriculum didn't cover. That may have been the point. A world presented in two rigid columns with boys on one side, girls on the other, was good enough for a teenager.

The school divided the classrooms that way, too. The female teachers took girls into one room, male teachers herded the boys into another, as if they were training us for separate destinies. Maybe that was also true.

At the time, I didn't question it. I couldn't imagine another way. The assumption was that everyone would grow up, marry someone of the opposite gender, and start a family. Anything beyond that was unspoken or deliberately suppressed. For those who didn't fit that mold, there was no language, no validation, and no place in the lessons.

It's only much later, watching how conversations around gender and sexuality have expanded, that I can see how much was missing. Those silences shaped us as much as the information our teachers taught us. By dividing us, by keeping the spectrum of human experience out of view, the system quietly told us what was acceptable and what wasn't. I believed that for a long time.

*******

Mr. Contos didn't cover the topic of contraception in class. In the 1960s, society wrapped sex and birth control in a thick layer of taboo. Nobody, including parents, teachers, and certainly not ministers on Sunday morning, talked about "it." If the subject came up at all, it was whispered, coded, or cloaked in nervous laughter.

Prophylactics were the only form of contraception available to most people, and even those carried an aura of shame.

The Pill was beginning to appear in the early 1960s, but it was controversial, and unmarried women often couldn't get a prescription. Contraception itself was legally restricted in some states until the Supreme Court's *Griswold v. Connecticut* decision in 1965 struck down bans on birth control for married couples. Even after that, the cultural climate lagged behind the law. Respectable people weren't supposed to need contraception, or at least, not to admit it.

I learned about birth control at the Bowlerama bowling alley, within walking distance of my house. Some of the neighbor kids stopped by to play pinball after school. Mounted on the restroom wall were vending machines from which condoms could be purchased for a quarter or fifty cents. The machines were the gateways through which young men and women navigated the line between curiosity, rebellion, and the fear of being found out. The secrecy itself was a lesson: sex was something to be hidden, controlled, and contained. And for those of us coming of age in that time, it shaped how we thought about our own bodies and the cost of intimacy.

I cranked a quarter or two into the machines. The little box dropped out, sometimes cellophane-wrapped, sometimes not. The plain ones came dusted with white talc. The ones with spermacide were greasy. The purchase was a risky act of confession that risked my reputation if the wrong person saw me. It wasn't a purchase like a pack of baseball cards, it was a public admission of private intentions: wishful thinking, in my case.

Rubber companies marketed their wares to men as devices that gave their partners pleasure, with no mention of birth control. Seems like some small print referred to "prevention of disease." The decals adhered to the tall, white-enameled steel dispensers, advertising images of condoms with bumps and ridges, as well as line drawings of seductive women. Big padlocks secured the vending machines.

I was going through my dad's dresser drawer, looking for a pair of cuff links in his jewelry box. In the back was a box of Trojan condoms, each neatly rolled and packed with a paper sleeve. I didn't dare bother them. They were available for purchase from behind the counter at the drugstore.

Another time, I was heading to the community swimming pool and pulled out a couple of beach towels. Mom must have wrapped one around an oblong cardboard box. I thought it was a forgotten Christmas present. I wasn't sure what the contraption was and looked up some of the words in the dictionary, and learned the contents turned out to be my mom's diaphragm and a tube of spermicide.

My second time sitting through this movie, I still felt disempowered. My parents encouraged me to participate in outside activities so I could meet new people, maybe a few girls, even though I may not have been able to clearly see them.

# Chapter 28

# Bad Eyes: Coke Bottle Glasses

One reason I liked to get on base by walking when I played Little League ball was that I couldn't see the pitches coming at me. I couldn't see a curveball break, and I ducked away. I couldn't help but believe that my impaired vision caused some of the injuries I sustained as an elderly first grader.

Until I was in Miss West's fifth-grade class, nobody realized my eyes were going bad. My mom had poor eyesight and wore glasses. My dad had perfect vision. A rite of passage for him was having to wear readers.

Some of my friends made fun of their classmates with glasses. Just what I needed, one more negative thing to cause bullies to notice me.

"You sit at the front of the class, so the teacher will think you're attentive," Mom encouraged. She wanted me to be the best Japanese American "Model Minority" student, which meant being good and raising my hand to answer every question.

"Anything good you do won't be noticed. Anything bad will reflect on not just you but our family," Mom warned. Guilt overrode my self-consciousness. Sitting at the front, my near-sightedness went unnoticed. My fifth-grade teacher, Miss

West, was the first to mention to my mom and dad at a parent-teacher conference that she suspected I was having trouble with my vision.

It wasn't until Miss West asked me to write something on the blackboard and I pressed my nose up against the slate that it became evident that I couldn't see past the length of my arm very clearly. My face was pressed nearly against the pages when reading at my desk.

Dr. Johnston was our family eye doctor. His family and mine went to the First Presbyterian Church. His son, Randy, was in my class, but he was a year younger than I, having skipped a grade.

I went in for my first eye exam and didn't know what to expect. The first step was to read the eye chart. I didn't want to flunk and was uneasy about being quizzed about which letters I could read.

I then sat in the examination chair. Having cold drops for the first time was also a surprise when the medical assistant dripped a drop into each of my eyes. Dr. Johnston walked into the room wearing a shirt and tie under a long white lab coat. He had a booming voice, indicative of his singing bass in the church choir.

"Looks like you have a scar on your right cornea," he said while pointing a penlight through my iris. Nobody had an explanation for the flaw. One theory was that Dr. Gramlich poked me in the eye at birth. Another was that it was a congenital disability. The latter reason proved to be a good conversation starter.

"Which is clearer, one or two?" Dr. Johnston asked while I was confused by the subtle differences in prescription choices posed by a piece of equipment called a phoropter. "Which is clearer, two or three?"

After it was all said and done, I returned to the office and picked up my first pair of glasses in the fall of my 5th-grade year. They were a plastic version of the Ray-Ban Wayfarer, with the top of the frame resembling a tortoiseshell design, and the bottom featuring a clear plastic rim that held the lenses in place. Every boy in school with glasses had similar frames. There weren't many choices.

I remember it was the fall because there was a room where we watched movies and film strips, and it had big windows that faced East 10th Street. The front yards across from the school featured cottonwood foliage, which was a mix of yellow and green.

When I looked across the street, I had never noticed that there were individual leaves. I stared through my glasses, then pushed them down on my nose, amazed at the difference.

I later learned that my left eye was 20/400, and my right was 20/40 and uncorrectable to 20/20 because of the flaw in my cornea.

The school boundary changed at the end of my kindergarten year. My parents wanted me to continue at Fairview Elementary School. Sister, Lori, would be in school the following year.

During the summer of 1960, they sold some investment land and purchased our new ranch-style house in the Cole Addition suburbs in East Cheyenne. A retaining wall made of concrete blocks was between our place and the McCulloughs to compensate for the hill.

In the 1960s, one of my favorite TV shows was *Combat!*, set during World War II. The stories were about an American outfit fighting the Nazis in Europe, led by Sgt. Saunders and Lt. Hanley. In one episode, the troops jumped over a wall chasing the Nazis in France. Not to be outdone, one of the neighbor kids and I decided to vault over the lower part of the retaining wall.

We chose not to hurdle because the drop was three feet. My friend took a run, placed his hands on the wall, and swung his feet around over to the other side. I followed and banged my forehead on the edge of one of the concrete blocks.

Afterward, I wondered if my hands slipped or if I had second thoughts mid-flight. More likely, I couldn't see where I was going. At that time, poor vision wasn't an obvious explanation. The next thing I knew was lying there on my back, bleeding profusely from a wound above the bridge of my nose, right between my eyes. My friend fled to get help.

My dad found me on the ground at the bottom of the wall and then carried me out. He loaded me into the backseat of our white-over-turquoise Pontiac two-door sedan. My mom had me cradled on her lap with an aluminum pot filled with water. She daubed the blood. My eyes were closed, but I could hear the water wringing out of a dish towel echo into the pot.

We drove to Memorial Hospital on Evans Avenue. The next thing I knew was lying on a gurney in the ER, where Dr. Cohen stitched me up with three black thread sutures.

My accident was the talk of the neighborhood. School started the following Monday. My first-grade nickname was "Butterfly" after the bandage that covered the wound.

Paying for medical bills was something that never crossed my mind. My dad made $10,000 per year. Mom didn't work. Medical costs were reasonable. The cost of childbirth in the 1950s was less than $200. The need for health insurance was low. I read that health insurance covered only 25 percent of medical payments.

The health insurance industry experienced significant growth during the 1960s, primarily due to the post-World War II suburban expansion, driven by a housing boom facilitated by the G.I. Bill, which provided easy home financing and veteran medical benefits.

I enjoyed the sympathy my classmates offered me and the "get well soon" gifts my grandparents gave me. The attention ended a few weeks later when Dr. Cohen plucked out the black thread from my head. He placed them in a small vial and handed them to me.

My first stitches ended up among my mom's prized keepsakes, which she kept in one of her jewelry boxes, along with locks of hair I whacked off the top of my head when I experimented with scissors.

# Chapter 29

# Childhood: I'm Lucky I Survived

Other than congenital poor vision and crooked teeth, I was in pretty good health for an aging grade-schooler. There were no vaccinations for infectious diseases like measles, chickenpox, and mumps in the 1950s and 1960s.

Between 1948 and 1955, several paralytic poliomyelitis epidemics broke out worldwide. U.S. public-health agencies reported roughly 16,000 polio deaths per year by the mid-1950s. In 1955, Dr. Jonas Salk licensed an inactivated vaccine made from killed polio virus strains. Eight years later, the oral, live-attenuated vaccine developed by Dr. Albert Sabin was approved. There was a rivalry: Salk's version was more expensive and time-consuming, a useful stopgap, while Sabin's was lower-cost and easier to administer.

Despite two vaccines, the virus hadn't disappeared. Many people didn't have access or chose not to be vaccinated; nearly five million children, many of whom were five years old or younger, in poor urban areas, missed out. In response, President John F. Kennedy signed the Vaccination Assistance Act of 1962, which transferred federal funds to the states for mass polio and DPT immunization efforts, thereby expanding the reach of these campaigns.

My family participated when I was in the 5th or 6th grade. We met at my grandparents' house on the Southside of Cheyenne on a "Sabin Sunday" before walking to the fire station. The Southside was one of the poorer areas of Cheyenne and a target for the program. We didn't have to prove anything or make an appointment. We stood in line while a volunteer brought a tray of paper cups holding sugar cubes infused with a drop of the pink oral vaccine.

A vaccination for chickenpox was unknown when I was in my 80s during the 1st and 2nd grades. Contracting childhood diseases was a badge of honor. My suburban Cole Addition Eastside neighborhood in Cheyenne was a close-knit community. That intimacy meant disease spread quickly.

When a bug moved through Fairview Elementary, attendance could plunge. Parents compared notes, and as with chickenpox, moms organized intentional "play dates" so kids would all be exposed at once and "get it over with." I went to one of those infection parties and came down with a mild case.

"It's better you get it now," Mom said. "If you get it as an adult, it's very bad." Scientists at the time didn't yet understand that the chickenpox virus could remain latent and later cause shingles.

Vaccinations felt barbaric. I got my first penicillin shot when I was small. The needle seemed as long and sharp as an ice pick. I could feel the medicine expand in my muscles. I wasn't a screamer since nothing hurt as much as the time my ankle snapped playing baseball, but those injections left an impression.

*******

Dr. Cohen was the one who administered that penicillin shot, but his main task was tending to my scrapes and injuries, and he conducted routine checkups that I came to like. He was a tall man with black hair and black horn-rimmed glasses, a bit bombastic and always smiling.

His office was across the alley from Carson's dental office. After school, Mom would drive me to the Logan Avenue office. We always arrived a little early, so I could look around Bunten Pharmacy on the corner, where I perused the forbidden *Mad Magazine* or spent my allowance on baseball cards before my appointment.

Dr. Cohen's exam routine was theatrical. He asked me to strip down to my briefs and climb onto the exam table covered with white paper that crinkled like a candy bar wrapper. His white coat pocket held a small flashlight, tongue depressors, and a little reflex hammer with a triangular reddish rubber head.

He'd thump my knees and elbows to check reflexes, poke my ears with a rubber bulb, and squirt a stream of warm water to flush out wax. He looked me over for scratches or bruises as a check against abuse. After a clean bill of health, there was a bowl of lollipops with strings suited for running without fear of a stick stabbing the back of my throat.

He made house calls, too. Once, when an intestinal blockage had me miserable, he and my mother set up a gravity-fed hot water bottle and administered my first enema. It was humiliating and uncomfortable, but he fixed my father's bag of green plastic army men, which softened the memory.

*******

Before kindergarten, I lived under my mother's care. She consulted with Dr. Cohen about any health issues that may have arisen. I think I missed out on meeting other kids because I didn't get out much. A few nursery schools existed, typically in large cities, but they primarily catered to middle and upper-class families. They weren't thought of as "academic," like a preschool, but more like safe places for play, socialization, and basic routines while mothers ran errands. For working-class families, especially in smaller towns like Cheyenne, early childhood education was almost unheard of. Kids stayed home until they were five or six and then went straight into kindergarten or first grade. I had two sets of grandparents and numerous aunts and uncles in Cheyenne, so childcare wasn't an issue.

The prevailing wisdom was that regular schooling was enough. Childhood before then was supposed to be carefree. We played outside, helped around the house, and maybe listened to story time at the library or Sunday school. Developmental psychology was only beginning to influence education. Piaget's theories about stages of child development were filtering into teacher training, but not yet into everyday family life.

By the 1960s, society began to recognize that early education could have a significant impact, especially on children living in poverty. President Lyndon Johnson's *War on Poverty* led to the creation of Head Start in 1965, which provided preschool education, meals, and health screenings for low-income children. The Perry Preschool study, for instance, demonstrated that children who attended did better once they entered elementary school. That was the first large-scale acknowledgment that what happened before kindergarten mattered.

*******

I was a product of the times. Breastfeeding had fallen out of fashion in the 1950s, replaced by cans of powdered formula that came with the stamp of science and modernity. Doctors and nurses encouraged it, hospitals handed out free samples, and companies like Similac and Nestlé advertised bottles as "better than nature." Popular culture at the time told mothers that formula gave their children balanced nutrition and freed them from the burden and the embarrassment of nursing in public. In that climate, Mom followed the medical wisdom of the day and bottle-fed me.

The unintended consequence was that my mouth never had to work very hard. As Nestor points out, breastfeeding builds muscle in the lips, tongue, and jaw. I would have suckled, chewed, and swallowed in a way that stimulated bone growth and made more room for my teeth.

Bottles required almost no effort. My jaw didn't expand the way nature intended, and when my permanent teeth came in, they crowded together like commuters squeezing onto a subway. My lifestyle as an infant and toddler laid down the roots of my crooked smile before I could even talk.

The same thing happened with food. The baby food industry was booming, another modern convenience for young mothers. Gerber baby food jars lined grocery store shelves. Mom had so many choices of soft, pre-digested peas, carrots, and applesauce mushed down to the texture of pudding that slid down without resistance. I never chewed anything of substance during early childhood. No gnawing on crusty bread, no tearing at a chunk of chicken. My jaw muscles stayed weak, my palate stayed narrow, and the crowding in my mouth worsened.

Meanwhile, cigarette smoke clouded my world. Both my parents smoked, as did nearly everyone they knew. Ashtrays sat on every coffee table, and cigarettes burned down between sips of coffee, with the air at home permanently hazy. If my obstetrician, Dr. Ralph Gramlich, ever worried about my mother's smoking during pregnancy, he didn't say much. In the 1950s, the medical profession not only tolerated cigarettes but also endorsed them. Doctors appeared in Camel and Lucky Strike ads claiming that their preferred brand soothed the throat or calmed the nerves. Fathers lit up in waiting rooms while their wives labored behind closed doors.

A few medical studies had linked smoking in pregnancy to low birth weight and infant health problems, but those warnings never reached most families. My mother probably puffed through pregnancy without guilt. The urban legends of the day told my mother that cigarettes steadied the nerves, and no one imagined that the smoke curling from her lips might be shaping me before I even took my first breath.

Taken together, baby formula, mushy baby food, and cigarette smoke were modern miracles of the 1950s. My parents trusted science, convenience, and the advice of doctors in white coats. They followed the recommended approach and employed technologically advanced methods in child rearing. Yet those choices left me with crooked teeth, a weaker jaw, and maybe even weaker eyesight. It's funny how the shortcuts of one generation become the cautionary tales of the next.

*******

My mom said that one of her friends had a case of the "nerves." I didn't know what she meant, but to my limited infantile knowledge. Obstetricians had a ready-made solution. They prescribed sedatives, like candy, a way to take the edge off without anyone really talking about what was going on inside.

It was part of the culture of the time. Mom wasn't encouraged to admit she was overwhelmed, and men weren't encouraged to ask for help. The message was simple: be a good wife, raise good children, and don't make a fuss. If the strain of it all showed through the cracks, a doctor could write a prescription and smooth it over.

I wondered what it must have been like for my mom and the women of her generation. Even if she never struggled with depression, she lived in a world where mothers who did, society didn't give them a safe place to say so. Instead, doctors handed them a prescription and expected them to keep smiling.

# Chapter 30

# Happy Ending:
# What a Way to Go

Living my life backward has been a strange and exquisite experiment unspooled in reverse. My fingers pulled a piece of twine back until the knot at the beginning revealed itself. After 89 years and now an infant, I could hardly be more at peace. I couldn't wait for the end to come.

On May 2, 1953, Dr. Gramlich oversaw my birth. I was nearing the end, while at the beginning. Obstetric medicine was different in the 1950s. The tools were simpler: stainless steel forceps, stethoscopes, and heavy glass syringes. The medical staff took the sterilization of their workspace and tools seriously. Hospitals boiled and autoclaved their instruments, although antibiotics were beginning to be used to combat postpartum infections.

Many births still occurred in hospitals, but home deliveries remained common in smaller towns and rural areas. Pain management leaned heavily on ether, chloroform, or "twilight sleep," a combination of morphine and scopolamine that dulled memory more than actual pain. Fathers were rarely in the room. Society viewed childbirth as the doctor's domain and expected mothers to be passive.

Doctors poorly understood postpartum depression. To my knowledge, my mom didn't experience it. Some physicians dismissed "baby blues" as nerves or hysteria. Instead of counseling, women were prescribed *Mama's Little Helper*: barbiturates or tranquilizers such as Miltown or Librium in the late 1950s. The emotional struggles of new mothers weren't yet part of the medical conversation.

After I popped out, my parents named me Alan (Teresa if I'd been a girl). Coming out of the womb and into a world of cigarettes, baby bottles, and mushy peas and carrots for lunch was a significant life change. I had a tough time breathing air instead of floating in spa-like privacy. As an infant, I was introspective. I spent my spare time with Mom during the day. Of course, all my time was spare time. Our little home felt isolated from other young families, save for relatives and an older couple next door.

I expected to feel regret about how I had lived my life. What I would change if I could go back? I could have nudged one thing, tried to alter one outcome, but I chose not to meddle much. Why risk altering a lifetime of memories with a careless whisper? The Butterfly Effect was reason enough to stay the reverent course and not rearrange the past. It kept the pattern of my life intact, with all its accidental grace.

*******

My parents "planned" me. I had to wait around for my demise to happen for seven years after they were married. I could have been 96 when I died and was born back in '42. They were older than the parents of my peers. Mom was twenty-six, two years older than the average age a woman gave birth, when I was born the first time. Maybe that's why I always felt like an old soul who arrived fashionably late to a party already in full swing.

I remember them that night in 1952 as clearly as a photograph. My parents prepared for a special evening to celebrate the sixth anniversary of their first date. They first met in the Skyline Nisei Club, a group formed by returning members of the 442nd Regimental Combat Team after World War II. Returning veterans of the all-Japanese team had gone away and returned with valor and new stories to share.

One of the club's rituals was a spring picnic at Hynds Lodge, west of Cheyenne. My father, Frank O'Hashi, was in charge of the Coca-Cola deliveries to the picnic. His family emigrated from Japan and settled in Ketchikan, Alaska, before eventually moving to Cheyenne, where they opened the Western Produce Exchange, a fresh vegetable brokerage business.

My mother, Sumiko Sakata, stayed at home when I was born. Her family also emigrated from Japan before moving to Cheyenne. Her father had retired from the Chicago, Burlington, & Quincey Railroad. Mom's father had retired from the railroad.

Mom and Dad were practical people. They didn't have a TV, but they enjoyed listening to music on the radio. They favored the Big Band sound, such as the steady rhythm of Glenn Miller's *"Pennsylvania 6-5000,"* and not the rock and roll favored by my contemporaries.

*******

That night, after the picnic, they ate quietly at the Little Bear Inn, the town's most upscale place then, and they returned home with the kind of calm that comes after a good meal. The house smelled faintly of Desert Flower perfume and cigarette smoke. The bedroom was dark. I was only a twinkle in their eyes, a possibility in a present that hummed with contentment.

There is something almost comic about dying into my beginning. I regressed to an infant and watched my muscle memory and speech unlearn themselves. Certainty dissolved into surprise. It made me tender toward myself. I have memories of the whole catalog of the loves and quarrels, small betrayals and larger mercies, the jobs I had and the ones that found me, the late-night conversations and the funerals.

Reversing through memories was a heavier burden. A loss I once wore like my watch became a lesson that slipped off my wrist when I wasn't looking. A challenging experience that once demanded an apology became a reverse pivot that led to laughter. Friendships revealed themselves after the first meeting. I felt lovers withdraw into the ease of early affection. If a regret reared its head, I took it in stride, acknowledged it, and then tucked it back into the nape of experiences that made me who I was, and later who I am.

I didn't live a life of reckless meddling. I watched the lives of others with curiosity, intervening rarely. There was arrogance in assuming that I could improve another person's path without flattening the hills that made them who they are. Besides, the delights of my experiment were not in changing outcomes but in observing them anew. Every sorrow became a seed of compassion, in reverse.

Some pleasures stubbornly remained pleasures no matter which direction time flowed. I always enjoyed the perfect cup of black coffee first thing in the morning. I liked listening to the Wyoming Public Radio hosts deliver the news each morning. These are the stitches that held my daily quilt together.

Then there was my final decision to die. Ecstasy is an image that people find either profane or sacred. For me, it was both. My last moments were lit by joy, by a human closeness that felt like the world's oldest vow. To end that way felt like tying the bow on my story that you might have read aloud, back to front.

If anyone asked what I learned from living a life in reverse, I'd tell them three things. First: small choices matter, but not all of them need your heavy hand. Second: compassion is the only currency that appreciates when spent. Third: don't spend your life polishing the lesson you think you need to learn. I learned some lessons meant to be messy, stubborn, and unique to me.

I am not sentimental about immortality. I have loved, screwed up, been forgiven, and forgiven others. I hold no grudges. I would not erase the stains of my life. They are proof I was here.

As the curtain closed, I felt gratitude more than grief for the people who kept me steady, for the music that steadied my rhythm, and for the unexpected kindnesses. I was grateful for the things I could not fix.

*******

Now I'm a twinkle at the end, only a notion in the vast and friendly world. My last and first thought before the hush and a new noise was that my universe had given me a gift: the chance to know the value of every single day, in both directions. I lived a good life in reverse.

Wise people say endings can be gentle. Mine will not be my soft last breath, but also the very first moment when two travelers collided and became a single entity.

I imagined the rush as membrane greeted membrane. Mom's egg was warm and waiting, Dad's single-minded sperm cell that wiggled its way forward. When the two cells met, nature took control. Surfaces folded, molecules rearranged, and the separateness became one. It wasn't carnal in the nasty sense. It was a loud thunderclap that marked a union that celebrated at the scale of atoms.

Inside my new, incandescent body, a cascade began with currents of water, a bloom of enzymes, the shutters of chromosomes opening and rearranging themselves into a future. Time narrowed and then expanded me as a single cell miracle. Two became one, and one became many. Now a zygote, I trembled, not with fear but with a bright joy of every road ahead, starting from a single glint in my parents' eyes.

In the Buddhist sense, I had become the nothingness between atoms in my old age. Death in ecstasy was my beginning. There was pleasure that wasn't about my new physical body but about my story.

Close the book on me and open it again with new instructions about how my life will unfurl after the first moment of life upon my death. The happy ending will be hard to beat!

# Epilogue: Death and Dignity

Living in reverse through time was insightful, even though I couldn't help but watch reruns of *Leave It to Beaver*. I did avoid watching *The English Patient* in 1996. Twenty out of 89 years weren't very productive. I was slowed down, home-bound, and needed assistance for the first 10 years when I experienced the pain of death and was reborn.

On the other end, the 10 years I spent growing younger and died in ecstasy were when I routinely dealt with the healthcare industrial complex under the care and feeding of my familial support system.

After getting the pain of death out of the way and ending up in the SSV senior cohousing community, my neighbors were a sound support system that complemented my qualifying for Medicare at age 65. The intentional community was similar to the neighborliness of the Cole Addition, where everyone looked out for all the children.

Another proof in point was when a friend named Neshama, who lived in the nearby Nomad cohousing community, contacted me shortly after my cataract surgery in 2019. She asked if I would make a documentary about Cherie, a terminally ill woman with multiple myeloma, a form of blood cancer.

I was interested in meeting Cherie because of my health-related close calls. Cherie was establishing her residency in Colorado so she could "die with dignity" in Boulder. In 2016, Colorado voters approved Proposition 106, the End of Life Options Act, which legalized assisted suicide.

I'm open to any story idea. Hemingway said to write one true sentence.

Like Papa, I don't want to run out of stories and prefer to actively participate in current and not-so-current events. I'm a doer, not a watcher. Without thinking about it, I hopped on this ship to see where it would land. In preparation, I watched *Farrah's Story* (2009). This made-for-TV documentary gives a glimpse into the life of former *Charlie's Angels* star Farrah Fawcett Majors as she confronts cancer, which eventually takes her life.

Before moving to Colorado, Cherie visited Denver from her home near Houston for medical marijuana treatments for pain relief. Then there was the experimental chimeric antigen receptor T-cell treatment. Cancer-immune T cells are a type of white blood cell that has been re-engineered in the laboratory to seek and destroy cancer cells. That was more effective than chemotherapy, but blood cancer prevailed.

After meeting Cherie and her support group members for the first time at Neshama's home in North Boulder, we drove to her attending physician's office. We splashed through a big rainstorm to Fort Collins for her initial consultation.

The doctor met us. He was a general practice medical doctor who also guided patients through the "death with dignity" process. We crammed into his office, where he explained the patient eligibility criteria spelled out in Proposition 106.

The participation criteria are straightforward. Cherie met all the requirements. In addition to being a Colorado resident at least 18 years old, a doctor had to have diagnosed her with a disease that would be fatal within six months. She was deemed mentally competent, capable of making her healthcare decisions, and physically able to self-administer the prescription drugs without assistance from others.

Over the next few months, I got to know the attractive Texan, her family, and the doctor. My first impression was that she was perky and always beaming. Cherie didn't look or act like she was very ill, but high doses of opiate drugs masked her chronic pain.

She had plans to do a few things before her chosen end time, which included celebrating her daughter Angelina's birthday and traveling to her son Matthew's college graduation. We planned for me to visit her in Texas. My trip to Houston didn't happen because her cancer progressed so quickly.

Cherie returned to Boulder after a long road trip with her son and daughter. We met up at the Nomad cohousing condo. She was worried about what her kids thought about their mother's healthcare choice. Upon their return, I had a chance to visit with Angelina and Matthew. We had an enjoyable chat.

She and I talked on the phone a few times and had one pretty good conversation. In the back of my mind was the Farrah Fawcett Majors documentary. It's one thing for a film crew to follow a celebrity, their friends, and family around.

We agreed that our documentary project was too voyeuristic as initially envisioned. It's pretty different to record the life of a regular person. Although there is a considerable amount of footage, I may complete the production if the right story emerges.

Cherie and I shared a common experience of facing death and talked about how life happens differently for everyone. Why did I make it out alive, and she didn't get better?

The night before she died, we sat together and talked briefly. We exchanged some small talk about her trip from Texas to Colorado, her kids, and whether it was okay if I shared her story someday. It turns out it's the punchline to this book.

I didn't feel like condolences were in order and felt that I should reserve those messages for surviving loved ones.

"You had a good run. You led a good life. You were a good mom. You've been doing a good thing about raising awareness about death with dignity," I said, giving her a hug and shaking her hand, before we parted ways. My presence when she swal-

lowed the medications prescribed by her doctor wasn't necessary to me.

The feeling I get about that sort of quality time, particularly
as an outsider, having a bedside view, is that it's a strange
badge of honor. I should make T-shirts that say, "I was there
when so-and-so took their last breath."

Cherie and I shared quality time along with Angelina and
Matthew when they visited Boulder a month or so before.
Cherie didn't say, but she seemed relieved when I reported that
both told me, a relative stranger, they were okay with their
mom's healthcare choice and would move forward with their
lives.

Taking one's life with a killer drug assistance isn't the least
expensive way to go, but it isn't as messy as other means, like
the shotgun Papa Hemingway stuck under his chin.

I'll never forget Cherie and her big smile and pleasant chatti-
ness. I am grateful we got to know each other, even if it was
only for a few months. Her experience gave me a better insight
into my mortality. The few experiences we shared had a positive influence on me.

*******

After living through my flirtations with death experiences,
I've become a bit of a hypochondriac. On the other hand, I'm
more fearless and empathetic to others who have trepidation
about the unknown. Our purpose while living for the short
time we do is to influence others.

That may include having kids who carry forward our values
developed and further influence the world based on their
unique experiences.

In my case, I didn't have children, but I relied on positive relationships with others, from casual to intimate, as a way to influence the future.

When I had my first brush with the Grim Reaper in 1976,
stranded in the Big Thompson Flood, I thought I was on bor-

rowed time and lived life recklessly, having too much wine, women, and song. I have many regrets from those days. If I were an alcoholic and following the 12-Step program, I'd be on a never-ending Step 9 mission to make amends with those I may have wronged.

It was 18 years after I lost my car in the Big Thompson Flood when I was returning from Sombrerete via Guadalajara in 1995. I cleared customs in Houston en route to Denver. The plane had a smooth takeoff, then suddenly dropped from the sky, sending the flight attendants tumbling down the aisle. The pilot had to make an emergency landing in Oklahoma City amid ambulances, fire engines, and foam trucks lining the airport runway because of a fire in the cockpit.

Nineteen years would pass. I was due for a harrowing experience that turned out to be the lung disease that nearly took me in 2013-2014. I half expected something worse would happen when I survived my deathbed. I imagined being on oxygen for the rest of my life or having a lung transplant.

My deathbed experience was the most financially uncertain time, as I had experienced a health insurance gap. KP would have canceled my policy due to my lung problem being a "pre-existing condition" if Congress had delayed Obamacare for a year. There's no telling how I would have ended up. My bills were a pittance compared to those of people with chronic diseases.

Had I died then, I would have been worth more dead than alive and saved society $98,000 in medical costs. I had Obamacare insurance. KP covered my bills, even though I had high deductibles. I have empathy for uninsured people.

Time is speeding up. My most recent flirt with death after being carted off a cruise ship to a hospital in Panama City, Panama, in 2023, happened 10 years later. My next healthcare emergency will likely be my last. If there's any consolation, I will have dodged another colonoscopy.

✱✱✱✱✱✱✱

I'll listen to other people about their bouts with pain, their busy, trouble-filled lives, and hope they get through whatever is bothering them. We all have personal challenges, and my frame of reference differs from those who haven't stared death in the face. I attribute my stoic attitude about minor problems of others to mild PTSD that I've developed after surviving my close calls.

Whether you live your life backward or forward, everything always works out in some way. One takeaway I gleaned from my Arapaho friends is that our experiences are neither good nor bad. Life just happens.

Doing no harm and being constantly at the top of your game is hard work. You never know when you might have a positive influence on someone.

-30-

# Disclaimer: What Do I Know?

hat do I know? I'm not a doctor, nurse, insurance agent, or lawyer.

I'm a patient and a customer.

Over the past seven decades, I've had many encounters with the healthcare industrial complex, and this memoir is simply a compilation of my personal experiences and reflections.

My biggest challenge from a creative standpoint was writing the story backward. Structuring the chapters with segues in reverse proved to be difficult. I still don't know if I have them right!

As for the data, I'm a journalist and check out three sources of information. How I interpret the information may be different than how you see the world. There are many opinions and perspectives on healthcare; these are mine. If you have questions or thoughts, I'd be glad to hear them.

You can reach me by email through Best Chance Media, an imprint of Boulder Community Media, at bouldercomedia@gmail.com

Alan O.

# About the Author

**Alan O'Hashi** and Boulder Community Media (BCM) work with community-based media producers, organizations, and socially responsible businesses to develop their content in a culturally competent manner. His work captures the nuance and complexity of self-identity, expanding the wider community's understanding of our pluralistic world.

Alan writes books and makes movies that are important, meaningful, entertaining, and inspiring. Through his books and films, Alan aims to have audiences experience the world from multiple perspectives, challenge their assumptions through storytelling, and gain a deeper understanding of their own individual identities and those of people different from themselves.

His writing and filmmaking explore the complexities of identity through his personal experiences with others. Alan's works are powerful explorations of the intersections of race, ethnicity, culture, nationality, and gender, and how these facets of identity shape our lives. He complicates the notion of what it means to be a non-white person living in the modern world and challenges the assumptions of others by sharing his experiences and perspectives.

By telling his stories on the silver screen and the written page, Alan invites readers and viewers to reflect on their lives and grapple with the complexities of self-identity in the present and the past, creating better futures. "I hope to create a more equitable society where people from all backgrounds are seen and heard."